Endangered Moral Values

HIPPOBOOKS

Endangered Moral Values

Nigeria's Search for Love, Truth, Justice and Intimacy

Sunday Bobai Agang

HIPPOBOOKS

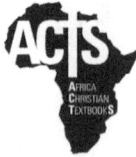

© 2022 Sunday Bobai Agang

Published 2022 by HippoBooks, an imprint of ACTS and Langham Publishing.

Africa Christian Textbooks (ACTS), TCNN, PMB 2020, Bukuru 930008, Plateau State, Nigeria
www.actsnigeria.org

Langham Publishing, PO Box 296, Carlisle, Cumbria, CA3 9WZ, UK
www.langhampublishing.org

ISBNs:
978-1-83973-210-2 Print
978-1-83973-707-7 ePub
978-1-83973-708-4 Mobi
978-1-83973-709-1 PDF

British Library Cataloguing-in-Publication Data
A catalogue record for this book is available from the British Library

ISBN: 978-1-83973-210-2

Cover & Book Design: projectluz.com

Nigeria is Africa's powerhouse. It is a place that is filled with opportunity and inhabited by a people of great promise! However, like many African nations, it is facing some serious moral and religious challenges. In this superb book, Dr. Sunday Agang offers a critical scholarly analysis of the current reality facing Nigeria and its citizens, which he then addresses against the backdrop of a set of theological and biblical moral principles. This book is of vital importance for Nigerians, and Africans across the continent, who are labouring for the "Africa God wants."

Dion A. Forster, PhD
Professor of Public Theology and Ethics,
Director of the Beyers Naudé Centre for Public Theology,
Stellenbosch University, South Africa

In this book you can hear a modern-day Jeremiah pleading with his people, with Nigeria. When the church, the economy and politics are excelling in corruption and tribal nepotism, modern variations of exile are inevitable. Africa's leading nation is heading to a moral abyss and untold suffering. However, the author believes that the people of Nigeria have the potential to realize their folly. Nigeria has the responsibility and potential to set an example and to help their continent to avoid a human and ecological disaster. To do so the church has to rediscover what it means to follow Christ and seek his kingdom.

Jurgens Hendriks, PhD
Emeritus Professor Practical Theology and Missiology,
Network for African Congregational Theology Advisor,
Stellenbosch University, South Africa

I commend this timely book for all Nigerians to read, study and implement the ideas set out in this book. This book should be read and studied by all Nigerian professionals training in our institutions of higher learning. This book is a must -read for Nigerians who hold positions of authority in Nigeria, especially politicians, civil servants and religious leaders. As a theologian and ethicist, it was gratifying to read this pace-setting book by a qualified, visionary and passionate colleague.

Yusufu Turaki, PhD
Professor of Theology and Social Ethics,
Jos ECWA Theological Seminary, Nigeria

Contents

Acknowledgements

Writing is a communal task. So, I acknowledge with profound thanks the many people whose ideas I have read and benefitted from, especially those whose words I have quoted or used in this book. Profound thanks go to my mentor, friend and senior colleague, the distinguished Professor emeritus, Ron Sider, who read my first draft and suggested a restructuring. Pastor Paul Crossly also read the first draft and made some valuable editorial comments, and I am grateful to him for that. I thank my students at ECWA Theological Seminary, Kagoro, (ETSK) whose stimulating and robust engagement with some of the issues addressed in the book also provided me with insights. Richard Stuebing, too, has been a precious writing friend. His willingness to proofread my work and to make suggestions for improvement has been invaluable.

It is also true that writing can only come alive when the environment is right. So I am deeply grateful to ETSK's Board of Governors and the ECWA Executive for approving my application for a sabbatical in 2018. I am equally thankful for the gracious provision of a Langham Writers' Grant and for the enormous contribution, both financially and emotionally, made by the Network for African Congregational Theology (NetACT), the Dutch Reformed Church (DRC) and the Beyers Naude Centre at the Faculty of Theology at Stellenbosch University. I must also mention those at the NetACT Weinhof House in Stellenbosch whose lively evening devotions in 2018 brought home to me many profound truths which I have included in this book.

I am most grateful to my new research assistants, Pastor Solomon Kwagheko and Dunason LA Dangbille, for all of their help in finding suitable material and sources to enhance the content of this book. The fruits of their work strengthened the arguments in several chapters.

Finally, I am eternally grateful to my lovely wife, Sarah, our beautiful children, our sons-in-law and our grandchildren who have supported me and prayed for me throughout the journey of this book.

Introduction

Why Another Book on Nigeria?

This book is written to celebrate the fact that the God of all creation has blessed Nigeria and Africa enormously, sustaining them by his power and intending them for his glory (Rom 11:36).

I love Nigeria, my country, and I love Africa, my continent! For many of us there is no place like Nigeria. It is a country of hundreds of millions of people and provides sanctuary for many of Africa's great men and women, among them theologians and clergy, scholars and intellectuals, politicians and diplomats, bankers and investors, entrepreneurs and business leaders, novelists and journalists, artists and entertainers, movie producers and comedians. Nigeria also has many professionals like psychologists and physicians, legal luminaries, scientists and medical scientists, to mention but a few. Besides these human skills, Nigeria is rich in natural resources.

This begs the question: Why then is Nigeria not able to provide the infrastructure that its people need? For years I have been haunted by the problem that Nigeria is so rich and yet is so poor? I ask this when I travel to other African countries. I ask it when I travel beyond our continent. On one occasion, when I travelled to the United States of America, my friends in Washington State took me to the Boeing company that assembles aeroplanes for the global community. I saw among them seven planes that had been completed for one of the African countries. I could not help but wonder why Nigeria could not sustain the Nigerian Airways enterprise. Why do things work better elsewhere? I wondered.

I asked the same question when I travelled on Togo's Asky Airlines and read how Asky Airlines has succeeded, winning many international awards. I asked it when I learned that Ethiopian Airlines has a fleet of 112 planes and has ordered 59 more. Why are things not working in Nigeria? Nigeria is not the only corrupt country in Africa, so I refuse to accept the explanation that it is purely because of corruption. I feel that we have to look elsewhere for an explanation for Nigeria's woes.

During a sabbatical in 2018, I spent six months in South Africa. Perhaps the perspective of distance enabled me to view my country clearly. One of the conclusions I came to was that Nigerians and many other peoples in the global community are slowly but surely losing their grip on their moral and ethical bearings. And without sound ethical and solid moral values, all Nigeria's God-given blessings will be distorted. Morality and ethics build a nation; immorality and a focus on carnal matters pull it down and render it weak and powerless. No generation of the human race can succeed in overcoming its moral and ethical crises without a self-conscious determination to live rightly in all spheres of life. No human generation is ever immune to a moral crisis. In our human history, the greatest empires that have ever existed collapsed morally before going into extinction. History reveals that no nation which joked about morality and ethics achieved immortality.

And history is repeating itself! Our world of today is threatened by moral decadence. Moral decline is fast becoming a universal norm. For those who live in the global west or north it is already difficult to think of the Christian church as a transforming power. Nigeria cannot hope to be an exception. We are part of the global south, which is believed to be the epicentre of Christianity today. Yet, Nigeria is facing these moral and ethical challenges too. What Nigerians need to acquire, therefore, is a new awareness that will help them see and infuse virtues, creating a national moral and ethical vision.

Meanwhile, our national moral crisis is bringing enormous hardships to the Nigerian people. I have tried to paint a picture of the current social, political, religious and economic woes of the nation. Nigerians (old and young alike) are crying out for an infusion of morality in every area of public life that will help us to recover the moral virtues of love, truth-telling, justice and unity that we sing about in our anthem and evoke as we say our pledge.

Those of us who read the Bible find within its pages narratives of human moral failures and the consequences thereof that resonate with our contemporary experience. A close examination of Nigeria's moral landscape will convince the reader that Nigeria is not very different from the world that the psalmist experienced many centuries ago. Listen:

> "Help, LORD, for no one is faithful anymore; those who are loyal have vanished from the human race. Everyone lies to their neighbour; they flatter with their lips but harbour deception in their hearts" (Ps 12:2)

The psalm goes on to outline a dismal picture of life then. Yet, Scripture also provides comfort. Then as now, God was at the centre of human affairs as both the psalmist and St Paul remind us. This is why the psalmist can say elsewhere: "The Lord is righteous, he loves justice; the upright will see his face." (Ps 11:7)

Our corrupt and distorted cultural and social attitudes cannot help us to arrive at a moral vision. We as Christians have the only key that makes this possible: the moral vision of our Creator God.

By and large, therefore, the focus of this book is on the art of living: How ought we to live as Nigerians? This book is meant to serve as a clarion call to contemporary Nigerians to rediscover their moral and ethical roots. It is my contribution to the spiritual, social, political and economic development and sustainability of Nigeria. In writing this book, I am following in the footsteps of the Nigerian founding fathers who believed in an indivisible Nigeria and who realised that only a moral and ethical vision characterized by love, truth, peace and justice can prepare the Nigerian people for this life and hereafter.

My prayer is that after reading these pages people living here will work hard to demonstrate to the rest of the world their deep love of both our country and our continent. It is my hope that this book will help to facilitate the kind of leadership which will promote moral purity and intellectual honesty and in so doing restore goodness, joy and peace.

Section One

Where Are We Now?

Africa's narrative is blotted with endemic corruption and other systemic injustices. Because it is a continent with such shaky foundations, Africa needs many different types of leaders to guide it on its path to transformation and technological development. However, the only leadership which will be able to reposition and transform the continent for the good of all its inhabitants is a moral and ethical one. There is a great need for leadership that is characterized by moral virtue. If Nigeria, the giant of Africa, were to provide such leadership, we would have 'The Africa We Want' as the African Union's Agenda 2063 (2015) expressed it.

1

Called to Meet the Needs of Africa

As we survey the situation in our country, we must remember that we do not live in a vacuum. After its independence from Britain on October 1, 1960, Nigerian leaders recognized the fact that if Africa wanted to survive as a united and prosperous continent, it was necessary for them to control not just their own area, but also to seek to settle disputes with other countries peacefully.[1] This far-sighted determination indicates that Nigeria has the God-given potential to lead Africa morally and ethically. "Due to its size and economic importance, Nigeria matters for West Africa, Africa, and the world."[2]

Over the years, I have watched with tremendous satisfaction how often, when African leaders are looking for someone to lead them on the continent, they approach my country, Nigeria. It is as if African leaders are saying "Give us a king who will lead us." Knowing that they are in no way inferior to those who were once their colonial masters, Africans want to show the world what they can do. This was one of the main reasons for the formation of the African Union (AU) on May 25, 1963.

These African leaders not only recognized Nigeria's potential to lead; over the years they have also provided my country with opportunities of leadership. Nigeria, therefore, has been asked to lead the African continent in many regional and continental forums. For example, in 1990 when members of the Anglophone Economic Community of West African States established the

---

1. "Nigeria @59: Nigeria's unsung leadership role in Africa." *Vanguard News.* https://www.vanguardngr.com/2019/09/nigeria-59-nigerias-unsung-leadership-role-in-africa/.

2. Ngozi Okonjo-Iweala, *Fighting Corruption is Dangerous:* The Story Behind the Headlines, (Cambridge: The MIT, 2018), xvii.

Economic Community of West Africa States Monitoring Group (ECOMOG) to intervene in Liberia's civil war (1989–1996), Nigeria was elected to lead the regional military campaign which rescued Liberia from its civil war. In 2019 Nigeria's President Muhammadu Buhari was asked to lead the African Union in fighting corruption and impunity in Africa. In 2020 the Community of West Africa also asked him to lead the region in its fight against the novel coronavirus pandemic. What is more, the richest man on the continent, Alico Dangote, is a Nigerian. Undoubtedly, Nigeria is a great nation with enormous potential.

Yes, the African peoples have been looking for an African country which can provide the necessary leadership in developing the continent's scientific, technological, economic, cultural, social and political potential. Many of them who have looked to Nigeria for leadership are enormously disappointed that this country is not providing what they need.

Given the size of its population and its intellectual potential, Nigeria should have been leading Africa to scientific and technological innovations, but I am aware that we fail to do so. I can't help but wonder whether Nigeria is really qualified to provide such critical leadership today. Increasingly it is becoming a land of moral gloom and confusion.[3] Our leaders have not been able to distance themselves from corruption and systemic injustices. Both Christians and non-Christians find it extremely difficult to live a life characterized by love and integrity. Goodness, peace and joy elude our citizens. And our failure affects others, as well as ourselves.

Among our leaders are some who are very disturbed by our country's lack of political will to step forward and provide the leadership that the continent requires if it is to reposition itself globally. During the fight against the novel coronavirus, for instance, many of our leaders felt that Nigeria should have provided significant scientific and technological leadership for the continent. Nigeria should have been at the forefront of developing integrated medicine or even a vaccine that could have weakened the impact of the virus. To provide such leadership this country needs to demonstrate that it believes in truth-telling, love, justice and honesty. Without these moral and ethical roadmaps, Nigeria cannot lead Africa forward.

It is in no small measure due to corruption and criminality that sixty percent of the population of the continent still live below the poverty line. Even in Nigeria every social stratum, every layer of society, is fouled by

---

3. Amujuri, B.A., Agu, S.U. & Onodugo, Ifeanyi Chris, "Is Nigeria's Claim of Leadership Role in Africa a Myth or Reality"? *International Journal of Multidisciplinary Research and Development,* 2/7 (2015): 343–353. http://www.allsubjectjournal.com/download/1043/2-6-33.pdf.

corruption. Criminals act with impunity and criminal activity is rife both among the upper classes and among the ordinary citizens. As in so many other countries across the global village, things in Nigeria are morally and ethically chaotic. Much of our daily life is spent figuring out how to survive in a world of diminishing returns.

Of course, our leaders may be acting on the assumption that it has been said that "government cannot legislate morality." But we know that is a myth. What about our constitution, that bible of democracy?[4] What about our other government public policies? Are they not moral pronouncements aimed at creating order, justice and freedom?

Yet I remain convinced that Nigeria has the potential to provide Africa with moral and ethical leadership. But it is one thing to have the potential; it is a completely different ball game to realize that potential.

---

4. Ofem Oboma, on *News* on Nigerian Television Authority (NTA) International, 12 June, 2020, at 7:00.

2

Nigeria and Globalization

We must begin our examination of Nigeria's situation by recognizing that Nigeria's moral crisis is not something totally exceptional. We live in the age of 'globalization,' and what happens in Nigeria is a reflection of what is happening elsewhere in the world.

This modern concept of globalization means that the human race sees itself as a single community. In many respects, this perspective is both theologically and scientifically correct. The Bible and science agree that all life on the planet Earth is interconnected. As I have pointed out elsewhere, I am very positive and optimistic about globalization. However, my observation over the years had led me to believe that there are two sides to this phenomenon. It has brought both tremendous blessings and huge problems.

Let us consider the blessings first. Clearly modern scientific and technological revolutions have made it possible for the human community to be a truly global village.

> Globalisation has brought enormous improvement in living conditions of developing countries. Statistics from the World Bank show that the world has been recording a massive improvement in living standards to the extent that [E]xtreme poverty has been reduced by 35% since 1990.[1]

The World Bank report states that:

> Globalization has spurred the spread of new technology, helping to make economies greener and more productive. Globalization has helped to reduce gender wage discrimination and given new

---

1. Agang, "Globalisation, Corruption and Terrorism: The Nigerian Experience", Agang, Pillay & Jones, eds., *Multi-Dimensional Perspective*, 46.

opportunities to women. Globalization has improved the quality
of management in firms and the working conditions for people.[2]

Our world has truly become a global village and information about what is
happening in one part of the world is transported to other parts. While that is
a blessing, especially when so many of our children live far away, globalization
is not all good.

> This reality must not be allowed to overshadow the fact that the
> world is still significantly and unprecedentedly divided between
> what are known as "developed' and "developing" economies.
> The flow of globalisation is like a vast river, with some countries
> sailing prosperously in massive ships in midstream while others
> struggle in canoes and rafts on the edges – and watch their people
> drown. . . .
>
> Despite its vast natural resources, including its vast population,
> Nigeria is still struggling to launch as a ship in the global river.
> There are many reasons for this, including Nigeria's inability
> to produce and export finished products. Our dependence on
> exporting raw materials is in part the result of colonial economic
> structures. Despite efforts to diversify the economy in the 1950s
> and the early 1960s, we still rely on exporting raw materials and
> have to buy finished goods from foreign industrialised nations at
> an exorbitant price.[3]

Most terrifyingly, Nigerians are the unsuspecting victims of a global context
in which modern civilisation is at risk. In his endorsement of Peter Kreeft's
book *Back to Virtue: Traditional Moral Wisdom for Modern Moral Confusion*,
Scot Hahn writes, "Christians live in a modern (or a postmodern) world where
we have reduced all virtues to one: being nice. And, we measure Jesus by our
standard instead of measuring our standard by Him."[4]

Peter Kreeft accurately asserts that the world "no longer seem to know
what vice and virtue are." He goes on to say,

> The most terrifying things (other than demons) ever to appear
> on our planet—thermonuclear bombs—have done a wonderful
> thing, a thing all the moralists, preachers, prophets, saints, and

---

2. World Bank Report, February 2019. https://velocityglobal.com/blog/globalization-benefits-and-challenges/.

3. Agang, "Globalisation, Corruption and Terrorism", 44.

4. Kreeft, *Back to Virtue, back page.*

sages in history could not do: they have made the practice of virtue a necessity for *survival*.[5]

Civilisation, he argues, consequently needs help now more than ever.

For exactly at the time when the fatal knowledge of how to destroy the entire human race has fallen forever into our hands, the knowledge of morality has fallen out.[6]

At this stage in our world's history the primary focus of many is not on the good and the bad. We live in a generation for whom morality and ethics are not issues that people think they need to bother about or pursue. Morality and ethics are not a priority: Most people are just concerned with how to 'make it' in life, with how to gain political and economic power, with how to be happy. As a result many people fall into the trap of idolisation and the pursuit of material well-being.

Of course the media plays a part in this. Although, as I have mentioned it can be a blessing, it can be also described as a curse in disguise because it distracts human beings from the most important thing in life. Every day it bombards us with information until we forget that, although there are many things to note or worry about, there is an immutable truth on which we can build our lives. The unshakeable truth is that God reigns over our lives. And when we forget that, we lose the rope which secures our existence on this planet. If we want to survive, we must develop the virtues that will enable us to practice morality as he intends us to do.

This means that we, the people of the Federal Republic of Nigeria, need to ponder the question posed by the authors of *Habit of the Heart* to their particular nation which is also facing moral crises: "How ought we to live?"[7] Roman Krznaric observed that the question is actually an ancient one but one which now needs to be posed "with a modern urgency." As we watch our national life being destroyed by rapid social, political, economic and moral insecurity and instability, we should take to heart what Krznaric writes below for it is part and parcel of the Nigerian social narrative, despite the fact that Nigeria does not display all the elements of the affluent West.

In the affluent West, society is changing faster than we can adjust to it. Online culture has transformed how we fall in love and

---

5. Kreeft, *Back to Virtue*, back page.
6. Kreeft, *Back to Virtue*, back page.
7. Bellah, Madsen, Sullivan, Swidler, & Tripton, *Habit of the Heart*, xii.

nurture our friendships. The demise of the job for life, and rising expectations of finding work that broadens our horizons as well as pays the bills, have increased our confusion about choosing the right career. . . . Moreover, the quest for consumer pleasures and material wealth . . . leaves many people yearning for deeper forms of fulfilment and meanings.[8]

Krznaric is right: "How to pursue the art of living has become the great quandary of our age."[9] Yet, Nigerians rejoice that it has become a capitalist and liberal democracy, and live to accumulate material possessions and political power. As a result, our generation, along with the rest of the world, is concerned not with living ethically but only with ethical discussion. We love to talk about ethical matters, but we have no ethical vision. The lack of moral and ethical vision causes an enormous moral vacuum. Kreeft suggests that therefore we are living in the frame of mind that St Paul described as, 'ever learning and never coming to a knowledge of the truth.' The consequence of this is that we are left living in a distorted and twisted world, a world that is morally and ethically upside-down. The problem is that we are pursuing and "searching meaning, security and fulfilment in an increasingly complex world."[10] The search for happiness, freedom and justice is not wrong. But we are searching for them in the wrong place: Without God there is absolutely no true security, true meaning of life or fulfilment on this side of eternity. Olusegun Obasanjo thus writes,

"The reason for being good is not found in this world alone because the true meaning and purpose of life, the sources of true happiness and joy do not reside in man. They are found outside self and outside man. They can only be found in God through faith, obedience, service and worship of Him and in love and service to humanity."[11]

For example, although the prophet Habbukuk was told, "The righteous shall live by their faith" (Hab 2:4 NRSV), and St Paul quotes him saying, 'From first to last, just as it is written: "the righteous will live by faith"' (Rom 1:17), our globalized world celebrates reason, putting sight above faith.

---

8. Krznaric, *How Should We Live*, ix.

9. Krznaric, ix.

10. Olusegun Obasanjo, *This Animal Called Man*, (Ogun, Nigeria: ALF Publication), n.d., vii.

11. Obasanjo, vii.

Because today we have idolized ethical discussion and choose to shape our own human-made values, we are now producing men and women who are full of malice and evil instead of sincerity and truth. Our moral values are endangered today because our generation like many generations of humans have continued to seek meaning outside of God. We have no clue that "the life and heart of man will remain purposeless and restless as long as man vainly seeks to find purpose in himself and for himself until he finds purpose, rest and faith in God." [12]" One of the reasons our moral values are getting eclipsed is not because we lack religion, which generally provides a moral anchor for life on this side of eternity. Religion equally supplies important answers for the meaning of life to the follower of that religion. However, we are experiencing increasing moral decline because, although many Nigerians generally portray themselves as being religious, they lack morality. What they practice is religiosity without morality.

Another issue at stake is that Nigerians live in the reality of a globalised world. They are therefore amongst those who have dangerously created a sacred-secular divide. Put another way, their globalized world has created a dichotomy between natural and supernatural virtues. Yet because God is the ultimate source of both and because we are made in the image of God, these natural and supernatural virtues are inseparable.

The Christian faith has failed to bring the much-needed moral and ethical light, gladness, joy and honour through a clear demonstration of God's power which could break down the walls of malice and evil and replace them with sincerity and truth. In fact, religion has become competitive and so no longer has much power to trigger collective action or to shape public opinion throughout God's world.

---

12. Obasanjo, vii.

3

The Character of Nigeria's Moral Crisis

Moral values do not just help a nation or society function; they are also an intrinsic part of its security, stability, progress and sustained transformation. They are the 'spinal cord' of any successful society. No nation or society which hopes and dreams for social, cultural, political and economic progress or transformation can achieve these things unless it takes its responsibility for its citizens' moral values seriously. Sadly our moral value infrastructures, systems and institutions are declining rapidly and therefore the situation in Nigeria is such that one feels that a moral 'state of emergency' should be declared.

This is not a recent phenomenon however.

> Ever since the involuntary amalgamation of various ethno-religious, geo-regional and political nationalities that made up the Nigerian entity on January 1, 1914, the country has been undergoing one critical socio-economic and political trial or the other. The issues and trends have been messy, characterised by uncertainty, conflicts (sometimes violent), controversy, compromise, and sacrifice. Resistance to the unity and cohesion of Nigeria has also dominated the Nigerian political scene over national question/national conference/restructuring, devolution of powers/true federalism, among others.[1]

---

1. Muhammad Fuad bn Othman, Nazariah Binti Osman, Isah Shehu Mohammed, "Restructuring Nigeria: The Dilemma and Critical Issues," in *Journal of Business and Social Review in Emerging Economies*, 5 (1), 79–98 https://www.researchgate.net/publication/335925475, 2019,

All the military juntas formed after every coup seem to have been manipulated by political pressure groups intent on securing their own economic, religious, class and personal interests.

This meant that they focused on military might and oil revenue development. Although they introduced structural and constitutional reforms in their attempts to correct the errors of the colonists, they neglected moral and social issues. Thus, although a 'War Against Indiscipline' (WAI) was initiated, it died as soon as the Buhari/Idiagbon regime was ousted. Then when the IBB and Abacha regimes allowed massive corruption that favoured the northern Moslems, other groups sprang up Obasanjo took over power in 1999 to protect their own interest – groups such as the OPC in the southwest, Bakassi in the southeast, MASSOP in the deep south, Boko Haram in the northeast and more recently the ACF in the north and the MBF in the Middle Belt. [2]

During his research visit to Nigeria, Karl Maier encountered a Shell public relations man, Bobo Brown, who was a former editor of *Sunray*, a respected newspaper in Port Harcourt. Bobo Brown described some of the factors that had led to Nigeria's moral decline as follows:

> Nigeria was suffering from a sort of national psychosis. Political and military leaders were corrupt, crime was seen by many as a legitimate avenue for advancement, and people in search of solutions were turning inwards to ethnic prejudice and religious bigotry.[3]

Brown further argued that,

> There is a complete split between power and moral right, and unless you have access to power, you have nothing. Everyone is seeking instant gratification. No one is prepared to think of the future.[4]

Maier notes how Brown laughed regretfully and exclaimed that, "Nigeria is the land of no tomorrow!"[5]

Nigeria's moral crisis is clearly broad and complex and the issues facing Nigeria today are literally legion. For convenience, however, I shall classify the issues into three broad categories: (1) socio-cultural issues or crises, (2) political issues and (3) judicial issues.

---

2. See class paper by Wadzani Mary Minso on Nigeria's Restructuring, May 16, 2020.
3. Maier, *This House Has Fallen*, xviii.
4. Maier, xviii.
5. Maier, xviii.

Moral Crises Arising from the Socio-Cultural Environment

Social and cultural matters breed many moral dilemmas. These crises centre around issues of ethnocentrism, tribalism and racism, as well as problems of family disintegration as a result of divorce, cohabitation and single parenting. Other issues which fall under this heading include the neglect of professional ethics and etiquette, drug abuse and misuse, the institutionalization of corruption and consequent institutional deterioration, and political domination. I have written about these elsewhere, but they are discussed in Section Two. [6]

Moral Crises Arising under the Aegis of Politics

The search for an orderly political society has eluded Nigeria.[7] Dan Agbese illustrates this as follows:

> Nigerians have a vast collection of colourful words and phrases they turn into political weapons as the needs arise. Some of these words and phrases are absent in political arguments in other countries.[8]

He cites the phrases, *mago-mago* and *wuru-wuru* which have been incorporated into Nigerian English. These two phrases are similar to the English words 'cheating' and 'fraud.' However, Agbese explains that, "Cheating and fraud are familiar criminal indulgences. Punishments for them sit in all laws in Nigeria and elsewhere." On the other hand,

> *mago-mago* and *wuru-wuru* refer to that rare and elusive degree of native intelligence skillfully employed to launder criminal actives in the context of political contests, losses and victories. A man can be arrested, charged, tried and jailed for fraud or cheating but the man accused of *mago-mago* or *wuru-wuru* suffers no such indignities.[9] (Italics added)

This indicates the level of political distortion. In turn, corruption results in despotic dictatorships, politics along ethnic lines, leadership succession issues, problems with democracy and with the multiparty system, civil wars and ethnic cleansing. The multi-party system in Nigeria does not reflect differences in

---

6. Agang, *Impact of Ethnic*, 91–95.
7. Mbah, *Government & Politics*, 120–121.
8. Agbese, *Nigeria Their Nigeria*, 135
9. Agbese, 134–135.

ideology as it does in other democratic societies, rather it is simply the result of multi-tribal groups in the nation. So a state is formed to create a political leadership opportunity for a few elite citizens. Agbese reminds us that this politicisation of the creation of states displeased one of the founding fathers of Nigeria, Obafemi Awolowo, who observed that,

> The naked truth about the position in Nigeria now is that, because of a number of factors, mainly subjective and emotional, partly environmental and historical, and to not a little extent personal, many leaders in Nigeria are implacably bent on having the territories of their birth carved out as separate states.[10]

He goes on to warn that,

> Those who advocate the creation of states only on the 'principles' of geographical continuity, economic viability and the like, are risking uncontrollable proliferation of states in the country. In the long run, we might find ourselves having to cope with well over 200 states.[11]

Other issues which reveal political moral decay include problems with regard to refugees and internally displaced persons, peaceful coexistence, land ownership and boundaries, population control, political ideologies and foreign policy, insurgencies and protests (anti-government, religious, or ethnic) as well as relationships between leaders and their followers and the relations between ethnic groups. A further source of political immorality is seen in the fact that political issues in Nigeria often interface with religion.

Moral Crises Arising within the Judiciary

Our lack of clear-cut awareness of national interests also promotes preferential and differential treatments in the judicial system. The judicial system is violated because of ethnic or tribal, religious and regional loyalties. Professional and judicial ethics are disregarded and judgments are at times determined according to one's class, one's political or religious affiliations or in terms of one's regional and ethnic associations. People often reflect their loyalties more than the national interest.

---

10. Awolowo, *Voice of Courage*, 168 cited in Agbese, *Nigeria Their Nigeria* 132–133.
11. Awolowo, 168 cited in Agbese, 132–133.

This moral decay leads to harassment, detention, the muzzling and imprisonment of those who fight for or who advocate human rights and civil liberties, detention without trial, torture and mutilation of suspects and gender issues.

Of course Nigeria, like other societies both simple and complex, has its unique or peculiar[12] values which it considers ideal and morally and ethically acceptable. Although throughout much of its history Nigeria has been characterized by misrule and plunder, the ideals of unity and progress espoused after the civil war, suggest that Nigeria has no reason for not prospering.

However, since independence, there has been an obvious ethical and moral decline in Nigeria, and as a result the leaders' efforts to improve our people's social, economic and moral lives have failed.[13] Rather than improving the people's lives, the elites, particularly those with political and economic power merely improve their own lives without doing anything for the masses, the poorest of the poor. What St Paul calls "the old bread leavened with malice and wickedness" has not been replaced with "the new unleavened bread of sincerity and truth (1 Cor 5:8)." The enormous economic resources God endowed us with are being devastated by our moral failure. The problems in our socio-political and socio-economic situations are compounded by a decline in moral and ethical consciousness.

Dan Agbese has observed that, although "we discuss in English we are actually speaking in our individual mother tongues."[14] By this he means that instead of acting as a nation, we see things from our own perspectives and "we find it impossible to settle basic issues about our country."[15] This has also contributed to the alarming rate of decline in moral awareness and moral behaviour among our citizens and this is why Nigeria is not among the list of countries that have succeeded in improving the livelihood of their citizens. Many writers have pointed out that the corrosion of (national) moral values has become a disease that is systematically eating away at our country, destroying the qualities and the potential of our citizens and leaders, both present and future.

---

12. Although, peculiarity can be used to refer to the national values of a nation, it is important to point out that most of these values are universally shared. What makes values unique however is the understanding, interpretation, application and limits of such values.

13. Cunliffe-Jones, *My Nigeria: Five Decades,* 29, 103–104

14. Agbese, *Nigeria, Their Nigeria,* 38

15. Agbese, *Nigeria, Their Nigeria,* 38

Many Nigerians do not realize that this is happening. It seems that men and women who adhere to moral and ethical principles are in short supply in the current social, cultural, political and economic context of Nigeria. Many citizens are no longer custodians of moral virtues. In fact, the few individuals who endeavour to uphold such virtues that once held our nation firmly are seen as oddities.[16] Moral values are disappearing among our citizens, young and old, in Nigeria today.

Nigerian society therefore has descended into an abyss of social, economic and political injustice where moral corruption and impunity reign. And the fact that there is little or no obvious demonstration of universally acceptable moral precepts among contemporary Nigerians is a tremendous cause of concern. Universally acceptable standards of moral behaviour or ethical conduct have been supplanted. The social vices have eaten deep into the moral fabric of the society and threaten Nigeria's constitutional aspirations and its promotion of "the good government and welfare of all persons in our country on the principles of freedom, equality and justice, and for the purpose of consolidating the unity of our people."[17] Nigeria is now regarded as a nation where we, the people of the Federal Republic of Nigeria – both the poor and the elite – swim in a pool of injustice, corruption and impunity.[18]

We, the people, take pride in our country's name – in all its various forms from the formal Nigeria to the informal Naija – regardless of the current social-political, economic, religious and ethical conditions of the nation, yet, although we share common beliefs, we are not able to share a common moral understanding. We fail to synchronize the various interests of our cultural and religious plurality. Sadly this means that our understanding of God's gracious gift of diversity is rapidly diminishing and that the desirable behaviours and attitudes that once showed our spirit of brotherhood and sisterhood are no longer appreciated. Instead, our sense of common nationhood is challenged.

Our moral corruption therefore extends to most institutions of society, to schools, families, workplaces, as well as our religious bodies. Despite the existence of a Christian community with a rich faith-based foundation, the blood of ethnicity is still thicker than the water of baptism. Perhaps it is significant that we used to teach morality and ethics, but that religious education is no longer a core course in our public institutions. Yet, as Faith Nkem Okobia,

---

16. Adedigba & Wahab, "Degenerated Moral Values," 249.

17. Constitution of the Federal Republic of Nigeria (Promulgation) Decree No. 24, 5th May, 1999, 15.

18. Cunliffe-Jones, My Nigeria, 29.

Mary I. Okafor & Justina N. Osajie have argued, it is religious education that builds a nation's foundations. They describe these norms and values as "the essential ingredients in the transformation of the nation" and suggest that the lack of them is "breeding moral decadence in the society." Consequently, they recommended that "religious education which inculcates good moral values such as honesty, fidelity to one's duty, love for one's neighbours and self-discipline" should be re-introduced.[19]

In Nigeria today, vices and immoral deeds are replacing virtues or moral values. The vices are taken to be the principles and the required standards.[20] Morality is meant to be the true foundation of Nigeria's unity and progress, but the present moral crisis has resulted in malice and evil: dishonesty, greed, intolerance, hatred, corruption, armed robbery, cultism, drug abuse, human trafficking, certificate racketeering, wealth without labour, indecency of all kinds, fraud, injustices, rape, disrespect for human dignity/life, assassination, kidnapping, ritual killings, adultery, fornication and so on.[21]

---

19. Okobia, Okafor & Osajie, "Reactivating Nigerian Norms,"
20. Matthew Hassan Kukah, *Church and the Politics*, 41.
21. Adedigba & Wahab, "Degenerated Moral Values," 249–50.

4

The Roots of Nigeria's Morality

Our lack of morality shows in our relationships. Nigerians confirm Olusegun Obasanja's assertion, "Man is a contradiction, a complex being, and a unique animal. On the one side of him are hatred, depravity, wickedness, transgression and sin, on the other side are kindness, compassion, love and humanness."[1] Thus, we have become the victims of hatred, division, exclusion, corruption, injustices, violent conflicts, kidnappings and unabated insurgency to name but some of our evils. This catalogue of moral decadence runs counter to the moral values that our national anthem and pledge encourage. We need to rediscover the moral blueprint for our country in its national anthem and the national pledge so that these can provide a moral agenda for the nation.

A national anthem to a large degree defines a country's identity.[2]

> A National anthem is a generally patriotic musical composition that evokes and eulogizes the history, traditions and struggles of its people, recognized either by a nation's government as the official national song, or by convention through use by the people. Furthermore, the national anthem is a self-identifying musical symbol of nation, country, nation-state, a people or an area with a self-identifying populace who regard themselves as a nation.[3]

In most, if not all, countries of the world, the national anthem is regarded as a symbol of national unity and a carrier of national values. In Nigeria the national anthem asserts the country's independence from the British empire-builders. In the words of Chinua Achebe, the anthem is "our very hymn of

---

1. Obasanjo, *This Animal Called Man*, vii.
2. Faniyan, "Stylistic Analysis."
3. Faniyan, "Stylistic Analysis."

deliverance from British colonial bondage."[4] However, the values embedded in the national anthem need some clarification if they are to help us to modify undesirable behaviours and habits.[5] Similarly, by clarifying our values we promote a spirit of brotherhood, cooperation and tolerance and allow for conflict resolution among citizens. However, we cannot simply expect the government to set things right. As Kirschenbaum notes, 'value clarification' is the responsibility of all citizens at all levels no matter what their background. Everybody can participate equally in this task.[6]

The National Anthem

All national anthems have social implications.

> Regardless of the country or region in question, their lyrics may symbolize power and sometimes victory.[7]

The old Nigerian national anthem (1960–1978), unlike most African national anthems which were composed by freedom fighters during their struggle for independence from colonial powers in the 1950s–1960s, was composed by a foreigner.[8] Before independence "anthems, particularly those drawn from Africa, were circumstantial," as the old Nigeria national anthem was. "They [were] artistic productions, poetry or prose written during the colonial period."

Our current anthem was not written during the colonial period, but some twenty-eight years later in 1978. The tune was derived from a local rhythm. And the words, according to Onditi, depict our "social, cultural, and political history," as well as our hope for the future.

Like most African national anthems, it was composed by a citizen. This new anthem was therefore motivated not by the need for liberation from colonial rule, but is instead a "solemn patriotic song adopted as an expression of national identity."[9] This means that the Nigerian national anthem is both a creed and a means of planting the idea of common nationhood in the hearts of our citizens, encouraging virtues such as loyalty, honesty, faithfulness, service and

---

4. Achebe, *Image of Africa*, 26.

5. Nwaubani, "Values clarification Strategies."

6. Kirschenbaum, "Comprehensive Model for Values Education and Moral education" cited in Adedigba & Wahab, "Degenerated Moral Values," 252.

7. Onditi, "African National Anthems", 3–20

8. Blake, Review article: "Voices of a Nation," 145–159.

9. Faniyan, "Stylistic Analysis." (See also Mohammed and Ayeni, "Political Leadership in Nigeria, 313.)

national consciousness. It was written to inspire "love or faith, unity, strength and courage" even in the face of adverse circumstances.

However, more than forty years (1978 to 2020) after the Nigerian national anthem was changed, we together with most African countries are still grappling with dangerous moral crises and anti-unity activities, lingering poverty, underdevelopment, protracted inter-tribal and interreligious conflicts and the politics of ethnicity.[10] These ongoing moral issues emphasize the need to examine the national anthem so that we can ascertain to what extent it has achieved its aims.

The national anthem is often sung during celebrations and programmes in an attempt to help Nigerians speak with one voice on national issues. This reveals that the nation's national visions, objectives, aspirations and dreams are indeed "embedded in Nigeria's National Anthem and National Pledge."[11] In spite of this, we can see that such aspirations "have all worked in reversed order most times." In the past, "the national anthem [was] second after the recital of prayers by the two dominant religions in our secular state." However, in what seems to be a socio-political reform, attention is now being drawn to the 'prayer' for the nation as contained in the national anthem. A decision has been made to ban religious prayers in interreligious, educational, or political programmes in favour of the second stanza of the national anthem. This has raised some concerns: How realistic is such a change? Will replacing prayer at public gatherings in favour of the national anthem help inculcate the desired values in the citizens? Is repeating the anthem enough to instil these desired values? These are questions that need to be considered urgently.

The first verse of the national anthem reads:

> Arise, O compatriots
> Nigeria's call obey,
> To serve our fatherland
> With love and strength and faith,
> The labour of our heroes past.
> Shall never be in vain,
> To serve with heart and might
> One nation bound in freedom
> Peace and Unity

---

10. See Onditi, "African National Anthems," 4; Agang, *The Impact of* Ethnic; Oyugi, "Ethnicity in the Electoral," 47; Noyoo, "Ethnicity and Development in," 58; Saha, "Ethnicity as a Resilient," 81.

11. Mohammed and Ayeni, "Political Leadership in Nigeria," 311, 317

The second verse is as follows:

> O God of Creation, direct our noble cause,
> Guide our leader's right,
> Help our youth the truth to know:
> In love and honesty to grow,
> And live in just and true,
> Great lofty heights attain,
> To build a nation where peace
> And justice shall reign.

For the purposes of our discussion at this stage, I shall focus on verse one, dividing it into its four separate statements:

Lines 1–2: "Arise, O compatriots, Nigeria's call obey"

The first two lines of this anthem are a call to all Nigerians at all levels to discharge their duty to their country. It is a plea that to all citizens to recognize the primacy of Nigeria and portrays the need to be loyal to Nigeria before anything else. It is expected that Nigerians will put the nation before their personal, tribal or religious interests. Loyalty is, after all, what distinguishes a citizen from a foreigner. The foreigner will always have split loyalties; a citizen, however, is loyal without a double allegiance. For the citizen, Nigeria comes first.[12]

Achebe reminds us that the old anthem was an "ominous beginning," a strange thing that "happened at our independence in 1960." He writes,

> Our national anthem, our very hymn of deliverance from British colonial bondage, was written for us by a British woman who unfortunately had not been properly briefed on the current awkwardness of the word tribe. So we found ourselves on independence morning rolling our tongue around the very same trickster: 'Though tribe and tongue may differ, in brotherhood we stand!'

However, Nigeria did not stand in brotherhood. Within six years of singing this old 'new' hymn which Achebe refers to as "strange and threatening", Nigeria was

---

12. Mohammed and Ayeni, "Political Leadership in Nigeria," 318.

standing or sprawling on a soil soaked in fratricidal blood. When it finally ceased to flow, we were ready for a new anthem written this time by ourselves. And we took care to expunge the jinxed word tribe." and replaced [it] with fellow citizens, that is "compatriots."[13]

Despite the fact that we adopted a new anthem, the word 'tribe' has not been banished from our national vocabulary. The tribe is still regarded as that which must define relationships and political affairs in our nation. Our national affairs still revolve around tribal and religious affiliations. Achebe goes on to say that,

All this self-conscious wish to banish tribe has proved largely futile because a word will stay around as long as there is work for it to do. In Nigeria, in spite of our protestations, there is plenty of work for tribe. Our threatening gestures against it have been premature, halfhearted or plain deceitful.

Lines 5–6: "To serve our fatherland with love and strength and faith"

It is not an exaggeration to say that the moral erosion in the nation is due to the failure of the nation to assimilate this call "To serve our fatherland." This promise also features in our national pledge and the oath of office taken by political leaders at all levels.

Yet we see moral decadence in all social strata of our nation: in the militancy in the Niger Delta, in the failure of federal, state and local governments to govern the nation effectively, in citizenship with its majority-minority questions, in the Islamic insurgencies and in the violence between the pastoral-cattle herdsmen (mostly Fulani) and the farmers especially in the Middle-Belt region, as well as other national ethical concerns.[14]

Such failures result in hopelessness as we watch the collapse of our value system. "Love and faith" are fundamental to the progress of Nigeria as a nation, but the present realities in Nigerian political leadership do not engender this. As Ehusani says,

---

13. Achebe, *Image of Africa*, 26–27; 34–35
14. Mohammed and Ayeni, "Political Leadership in Nigeria," 311.

Our political landscape remains dominated by primitive greed, hatred, bitterness, resentment, violence and crime.[15]

These characteristics have huge consequences. Mohammed and Ayeni comment that:

The labour of our pseudo heroes has been the masses being manipulated advertently or inadvertently to serve the ruling political leadership with heart and might to their own end. To state that Nigeria's National Pledge is a contradiction to the crop of leadership Nigeria has as a country is the fact.[16]

Achebe meanwhile points out that,

Faith is all right provided it is to be placed on something acceptable. It cannot be good in itself. Before we are persuaded to have faith, we must first ascertain the nature and worth of the receiver of our faith. We must ask the crucial question: Faith in what? Just as in the matter of unity we must ask: Unity to what end?[17]

The first heroes were united and strong in their fight for a nation and their fight was fuelled by their "love and faith" in Nigeria. If we want to progress, we must be like them. In fact we must do more. In our effort to move forward, love and unity must be our watchwords, but they must be accompanied by justice and honesty. As Mohammed and Ayeni observe,

The call 'to serve with love and strength and faith' is channeled to narrow self-interest as conflicts abound to amass the collective resources and wealth of the nation.[18]

Yet today it is the norm rather than the exception to put self-interest before national interest—if there is any national interest![19] Ogbeide recounts the following concerning the inquiries instituted by General Murtala Muahmmed's miltary government:

15. Ehusani, "The Role of Religion in the Nigerian Political System." *Daily Magazine.* Vol.1. 2001): 64. Cited in Mohammed and Ayeni, "Political Leadership in Nigeria," 319. See also Vaughan, *Religion and the Making.*

16. Mohammed and Ayeni, "Political Leadership in Nigeria," 319.

17. Achebe, *Image of Africa*, 33.

18. Mohammed and Ayeni, "Political Leadership in Nigeria," 318.

19. For a detailed analysis of such acts, see Siollun, *Oil, Politics and*; Ogunsanwo, *General Yakubu Gowon*; Okonjo-Iweala, *Reforming the Unreformable*, 81; El-Rufai, *Accidental Public Servant*, 155–238. For details on fighting corruption see Okonjo-Iweala, *Fighting Corruption is Dangerous*; Mohammed and Ayeni, "Political Leadership in Nigeria," 321.

Similar commissions of inquiry were consituted by the new state governments which resulted in resulted in the immediate dismissal of several corrupt officials, many of who were in turn ordered to refund the money they had stolen. General Murtala was assassinated after only six months in office . . . The killing of General Murtala [was] a setback to national development. One may want to ask if political leadership in Nigeria will ever be sincere with their oath of being *faithful and honest* to the Nigerian State.[20]

Why are Nigerian leaders not keeping their oath? What role is the National Orientation Agency (NOA) playing in ensuring that this call is heeded by all Nigerians at all levels? Surely the government should be attempting to answer these questions as they seek to deal with the numerous moral crises in Nigeria.

Lines 7 and 8: "The labour of our heroes past shall never be in vain"

Unless we serve our country with love, strength and faith, the labour of our past heroes will have been in vain. This section of the national anthem is an acknowledgement of the efforts and sacrifices of the past leaders or heroes who fought for the independence of Nigeria. These early heroes include both those who were alive to witness the ceremony in 1960 and those who died before independence. However we have to ask what progress we have made as a nation in our own task of building a just and egalitarian society, a prosperous and viable nation.

It is important to note that in the old anthem the singers remind themselves and others "about a bond of heritage that must not be desecrated: native land, brotherhood and common motherland. This is despite the differences in tribe and tongue."[21] Although the use of the terms "tribe and tongue" in the old anthem is considered a "strange thing"[22] the first heroes clearly recognized both their diversity and their common heritage. They are one in spite of the differences in tribe and dialect. In spite of such acknowledgements, however, Nigeria unfortunately "did not stand too long in brotherhood."

What was the problem? Didn't they serve with their heart and might? Or was their understanding of freedom and unity flawed by a lack of respect?

---

20. Ogbeidi, "Political leadership and Corruption," 8
21. Chukwu, et al, "Dialectics of Contradiction in," 232.
22. Achebe, *Image of Africa*, 26–27.

Lines 9–11: "To serve with heart and might one nation bound in freedom, peace and unity."

These last three lines of the anthem are a necessary reiteration of the call to serve with love, strength and faith. The emphasis here falls however on the three pillars of nationalism, "freedom, peace and unity."

These lines explain why we desire progress as a nation. Progress will enable us to ensure that our common destiny is continuous freedom, thus "bound in freedom." Although those whose freedom has never been threatened might not appreciate liberty, this liberty was valued immensely by people who had directly experienced colonial rule.[23] And we are tasked to remind and educate every succeeding generation of Nigerians where we were coming from and where we want to go. Nigeria must make every effort to tell the story of its struggles prior to independence to every generation of Nigerians. We must explain what life was under the colonial rulers and the struggles our first heroes had to gain our freedom. All must know that it is this freedom that ensures our peace and unity. This is why the new anthem proclaims solidarity on the basis of "the labour of our heroes past", while the old anthem merely emphasized "brotherhood."

Two values are added in these last lines: 'serving with heart and might to ensure peace and unity. This suggests that freedom might be easy to get, but harder to sustain. It requires "might" to sustain freedom. This statement is also reflected in the last line of the last stanza of the Chadian anthem, warning the citizens of Chad to remain watchful so that they can preserve their freedom: "Your freedom will be born of your courage." Onditi writes that

> Inter-regional similarities in the conceptualization of anthems are evident across the continent. For instance, the same themes of peace and protecting the nation from enemies also exist in anthems from Malawi, Kenya, Tanzania, Gambia and Nigeria.

We can see then that the lyrics of our national anthem present both harmony and tension as we seek to develop our Nigerian potential. On one hand, the anthem conveys the need for nation-building and peace-building. This should encourage us to pursue a harmonious process driven by the need to maintain unity and peace in our land. It should recognize the significant role played by God, by our ancestors (our "heroes past") and by natural forces (our "land"). On the other hand, the anthem reflects tension because there is no clear understanding of diversity. Prospects for a positive peace depend

---

23. see Turaki, *The British Colonial Legacy*; Turaki, *Tainted Legacy: Islam, Colonialism*

on a proper understanding of the elements of nation-building, such as God, unity, peace, human dignity and land as a source of food and prosperity. This means that "any attempt to conduct a social construction (developing theory of change) for peacebuilding based on the philosophies of national anthems"[24] will require us to develop a clear understanding of our diversity and our interests.

The National Pledge

In taking this oath, a Nigerian leader pledges:

> To be faithful loyal and honest,
> To serve Nigeria with all my strength,
> To defend her unity,
> And uphold her honour and glory.

Our pledge endorses the oath made in the national anthem. As we serve Nigeria with all our strength, love and faith, we pledge to do so with faithfulness, loyalty and honesty.

The concluding recognition of God in the discharge of this duty is a prayer. It is worrisome that on every public or official occasion Nigerians sing the national anthem and make the pledge of allegiance, which concludes with "so help me, God," although to many this is just an empty statement. Even after saying, "so help me God," Nigerians are preoccupied with materialism (mammon) instead of the God they call upon.

Although questions have been raised as to the identity of the object of this faith, the national anthem and pledge of allegiance remain a clear invitation for Nigerians to seek God above all other things. There are some who would like to see 'So help me God' changed to "So help me, god." If only they would realize that all of the things they are concerned and worried about are nothing compared to the Kingdom of God and the reign of God over all of life. If they did, perhaps the corruption and hypocrisy that we see today would be destroyed.

Mohammed and Ayeni quote the following:

> This National Pledge . . . is recited in schools during assemblies, [on] Independence Day, and [at] official government functions. As when reading a love poem, the National Anthem and Pledge are well based to bind us together in unity (Leonard; H. 1996).

---

24. Onditi, "African National Anthems," 16.

However, they also observe that this pledge seems unfortunately to have changed to: "I pledge to loot Nigeria my country, to be unfaithful, disloyal and dishonest to serve Nigeria, with none of my strength."[25] Achebe seems to confirm this when he notes,

> National pledges and pious admonitions administered by the ruling classes or their paid agents are entirely useless in fostering true patriotism. In extreme circumstances of social, economic and political inequities such as we have in Nigeria, pledges and admonitions may even work in the reverse direction and provoke rejection or cynicism and despair.[26]

A prominent Nigerian elder-statesman questions the choice of the "easy virtues" in our pledge and our motto "Unity and Faith." Easy virtues, he suggests "are amenable to the manipulation of hypocrites, rather than difficult ones [like justice and honesty] which would have imposed the strain of seriousness upon us." He also suggests that "'virtues' like *unity* and *faith* are not absolute but conditional on their satisfaction of other purposes. Their social validity depends on the willingness or ability of citizens to ask the searching question. This calls for a habit of mental rigour, for which, unfortunately, Nigerians are not famous.

Yet the pledge implies that a loyal, faithful and honest citizen should not covet or take another person's property illegally. "If the above scenario holds, looting of the state treasury is a negation of the oath taken by political leadership in Nigeria." Yet the history of Nigeria is replete with stories in which the national pledge was disregarded. No political era is exempt from this indictment. The military in the 1970s, 1980s and 1990s "worked in sharp contradiction to the Nigerian National Pledge." The history of governance in Nigeria overflows with evidence of contract inflation for private gain at great cost to the government. "It is a fact that the level of looting state treasury by the military during the governments of Generals Babangida (1985–1993), Abacha (1993–1998) and Abdulsalam (1998–1999)"[27] was alarming, contradicting the National Pledge and their oath of office. Nor can we exonerate the more recent democratic leadership. The establishment of agencies such as the Independent Corrupt Practices and other Related Offences Commission (ICPC) and Economic and Financial Crimes Commission (EFCC) suggests the perpetual

---

25. Mohammed and Ayeni, "Political Leadership in Nigeria," 313, 319.

26. Achebe, *Image of Africa*, 36.

27. Mohammed and Ayeni, "Political Leadership in Nigeria," 320.

nature of corruption in Nigeria. This is affirmed by Okonjo-Iweala who says that "By the time we began the economic reform program, Nigeria had become virtually synonymous with the word 'corruption.'"[28]

If, as Mohammed and Ayeni observe, the youth of a country is its strength, "how then [does] the political leadership serve Nigeria with all his strength when her symbol of strength; the youths, are wasting away in cities and towns and villages trying to get jobs that either don't exist or are reserved for children of the ruling class?" This is a crucial question of sustainability as hundreds of Nigerian youths die every year in an effort to cross the Mediterranean into Italy and eventually other parts of Europe. This is how the strength of Nigeria is being wasted. According to reports, one of the reasons that the United States of America has placed a restriction on immigration visas for Nigerians is because research conducted by the embassy revealed that 47% of Nigerians want to leave the country. The wastage of resources leaves nothing for an average citizen to benefit from, "hence the need for Nigerians to move out of the country [sometimes] by illegitimate means in search of greener pastures,"[29] leaving their once 'green' country.

There are other statements in the pledge that many Nigerians fail to agree on. The first concerns the promise to defend the unity of Nigeria. With the high level of corruption, favouritism and nepotism, bigotry, religious intolerance and hatred of all kinds, the desire for unity has become the preserve of the elites.

---

28. Okonjo-Iweala, *Reforming the Unreformable*, 81.
29. Mohammed and Ayeni, "Political Leadership in Nigeria," 321.

Section Two

A Closer Look at Specific Socio-Cultural Issues

I have already indicated that ethnocentrism, tribalism, racism and family disintegration are consequences of moral decline. We could also include under this heading the neglect of professional ethics and etiquette, drug abuse and misuse, the institutionalization of corruption and consequent institutional deterioration, as well as political domination.

When we consider, for example, the institutionalization of corruption, we realize that this arises from misconceptions and misunderstandings about the functions of tribe and religion as well as the fact that these have been institutionalized via the Federal Character Commission.[1]

If we could manage our cultural and religious plurality, Nigeria's grand democratic experiment would be applauded internationally. Nigeria, however, is not the only country in Africa to experience these problems. In fact, understanding the situation here can help us to understand the situation across the continent.

---

1. "Federal Character Commission (FCC) http://www.federalcharacter.gov.ng/index.php/about-us. See also: Joshua, Loromeke and Olanrewaju, "Quota System, Federal Character," 1–10.

5

Tribalism

When we consider, for example, the institutionalization of corruption, it is clear that this arises partly from misconceptions and misunderstandings about the functions of the tribe. In Africa, there are many consequences because political activities are influenced by a misunderstanding of diversity. Countries like Togo, Sudan, South Sudan, Liberia, Sierra Leone, Central Africa, Egypt, Zambia, Zimbabwe, Kenya, South Africa and DRC can all testify to the bitterness that tribalism stirs up.[1] Understanding diversity through the lenses of error, however, can mean that we simply end up promoting tribal or ethnic links rather than the national ones. Such actions have led to the fragmentation of the nation.

The evidence for this is overwhelming. We can look back at what we experienced in 1967 as well as in the history of our political parties. Certain nationalists' descriptions of Nigeria also provide evidence of this. For example, in Obafemi Awolowo's picture of Nigeria, he declares that:

> Nigeria is not a nation. It is a mere geographical expression. There are no 'Nigerians' in the same sense as there are 'English,' 'Welsh,' or 'French.' The word 'Nigerian' is merely a distinctive appellation to distinguish those who live within the boundaries of Nigeria and those who do not.[2]

Although Awolowo's comment alludes to the bigger issue of a national or official language as well as a common tradition, what he is saying impacts on the political life of Nigeria. Of course, his comparison is wrong because he did

---

1. See Zeleza, "The Causes and Costs of War in Africa: From Liberation Struggles to the 'War on Terror,'" in Zeleza (eds.) *Roots of Africa*; Marshall, *Conflict Trends in Africa* and Siollun *Oil, Politics and Violence*.

2. Obafemi Awolowo as cited by Marshall, *Conflict Trends in Africa*; Siollun, *Oil, Politics and Violence*, 11–68, 97–116, 127–149

not go back far enough in Western history. Even European countries once had many 'tribes' that spoke different languages. However, we can put that error aside for the ethnic situation he alludes to is actually a moral one.

Agbese points out that,

> Many of the Nigerian tribes had distinctive facial marks that made them truly unique. Some tribes even classified their tribal marks. Royal facial marks were distinct from those of commoners within the same tribe. Commoners dared not use royal facial marks.[3]

From what has been discussed, it is clear that, despite more than half a century of nation building, Nigeria is still driven by ethnic particularism, commonly known as 'tribalism.'

Scholars as well as some of our leaders are bewildered by the fact that tribal ideologies persist tenaciously despite the profound changes resulting from modernization and globalization. And yet they do. There is clearly still a need for increased cultural, religious and democratic understanding and mutual sensitivity so that we can engage more constructively with tribal groups.

Since the return to democratic governance in 1999 after about fifteen years of military rule, Nigeria has begun the difficult process of establishing a rule of law sensitive to local traditions. This included the re-adoption of shari'a criminal law in the twelve northernmost states of Sunni and Maliki heritage. Although the military showed some sensitivity to local traditions as it created states based on either ethnic or religious lines, there has always been a fragile relationship between the federal officials and the local leaders (traditional and civic).

This relationship was weakened by the fact that the liberal democratic model, on which most African states were founded when they gained independence from colonial rule and to which they continue to aspire, is founded on majority rule. The colonial concept of a 'majority' versus a 'minority' was, as it were, smuggled in to dictate our national affairs. And this concept of majority rule can destroy communities as it can lead to the domination of 'minority' tribes by so-called 'majority' tribes. Maintaining the balance between majority rule and minority rights has, consequently, in the decades since independence become the key national question in many African countries, perhaps none more so than in Nigeria.

Most people in Nigeria today see the tribe as one of the fundamental factors that militate against national unity and development and the emergence

---

3. Agbese, *Nigeria Their Nigeria*, 34

of a national consciousness or interest. The big question facing Nigeria today is therefore how to build national unity in the face of our widespread ethnic diversities and the competition for resources.

We need to start by defining the word 'tribe.' Yet even when we turn to the most comprehensive dictionaries, we get no help at all. Most dictionaries simply define a tribe as a tribal organization, culture, loyalty, social division of people, in terms of common ancestry, custom, belief and leadership, etc. But clearly this definition is inadequate. How can one's culture/custom or loyalty lead to national disunity? How can one's tribal origin constitute a reason for national failure?

Paul Iyorpuu Unongo rightly observes that mere culture is not what is at play when Nigerians describe the impact of the tribe or tribalism on national affairs as a 'cankerworm,' or as an 'evil' or as a 'sin.' Culture is not the reason that many people have come to believe that the concept of the tribe should be outlawed "permanently"[4] from governance. People are not calling for policies to regulate or ban tribal culture or tribalism. Rather, what they are calling for is a ban on using tribal links to allow either oneself or one's tribe to benefit to the disadvantage of others in the state or to the detriment of national interest.

This kind of exploitation is common in Nigeria when it comes to things like appointments, contracts, admissions, scholarships and employment. There are many stories of people who were denied jobs, not because they are not qualified, but because of their tribal affiliation. These stories show the insidious impact of tribalism and religious bigotry on Nigerian society.

Here is one such story: Amos Mun-Kadang[5] was the first child in his family and his village to leave his area in search of advanced tertiary education. Amos sat for the Unified Tertiary Matriculation Examination (UTME), which is conducted annually by the Joint Admission and Matriculation Board (JAMB). This is the required exam for any candidate seeking admission into any of the country's tertiary institutions. Amos wanted to study architecture, and he scored 210 in his UTME exam, well above the required 180. This was therefore a good mark for anyone looking for admission into university or its equivalent.

Amos then went for his post-UTME screening for admission to one of the universities in the north. As part of the exercise, one's original high school or official results are carefully checked to ensure that one is qualified to be admitted into the department of one's choice. Amos had all the O-Level requirements for the architectural department although some of his fellow

---

4. Unongo, *Say It Loud*, 54.

5. A fictitious name

candidates were deficient in English and other required subjects such as Mathematics or Physics.

Yet it was at this point that his problem arose. All applicants are required to complete a biodata form before the UTME screening exercises in Nigeria. One is required to state one's religion, state, local government area and tribe, among other things. This is why Amos's details were known to the head of department and the head of department chose to favour those with whom he shared tribal and religious affiliations.

Amos and over 20 other candidates who did not meet these religious and ethnic requirements were not accepted. The admitted candidates included some who met the academic requirements, but there were others who did not measure up at all. Very few of those who did not meet the ethnic and religious requirements were admitted, but some who should have been admitted were replaced by others with the right ethnic and religious affiliations, even though they were not competent academically. Such candidates were merely required to catch up in the various subjects although their previous performance should have precluded them from being admitted.

When the announcement was made that they had not been accepted, Amos and the others who did not meet the unwritten yet powerful requirements of tribal and religious affiliations were asked to pay huge sums of money in order to be considered for admission. Their female counterparts were asked to pay either the required amount or o pay 'with what they had.' This implied sexual favours. Amos and the other unadmitted candidates were warned, however, that payment by whatever means would not gain them admission to their chosen department. Instead they would be admitted to study geography or some other discipline.

At this point Amos found himself in a precarious situation. He could neither afford to pay the required amount for the admission he merited, nor did he want to study geography. What is more, he knew that admission was not guaranteed even after payment. Amos became terribly demoralized. He eventually returned to his village, putting an end to his dream of higher education and to the dreams of his family and his village.

Amos is not an isolated case in Nigeria's education system. Stories about how one's tribe became a hindrance to one's self-development abound. Many Nigerians have been victimized in similar or even worse circumstances. There are numerous cases of educational admission committees asking for under-the-table payments before students are admitted, or before they receive their results and their grades. Such corrupt practices in the educational sector mean that the provision of quality education is poor. Yet education could remedy some of the problems that Nigeria faces.

Of course, the game of using tribal affiliation to break a rule and so to gain advantage is played by both the minority and majority tribes in Nigeria. The 'minority' use it as a means of gaining political, educational and economic freedom, while the 'majority' use it to further enforce their dominance.

We saw from the story of Amos that usually, a minority is distinguished from the majority group in the same society as a result of some kind of registration form that requires one to list one's personal biodata, such as one's name, religion, tribe, language and age. Once these details are known, people can be categorized and can become subject to exclusion, discrimination and other differential treatment.

In Nigeria's early days, both civilian and military policies failed to integrate the peoples. When independence was won in 1960 the regions were not homogeneous ethnically. The Hausa–Fulani, Yoruba and Igbo respectively dominated the northern, western and eastern regions of the country, numerically. These "are usually referred to as the majority ethnic groups. Others such as the Edos, Urhobos, Ibibio/Efik, Ijaws and so on in the South and the Gwaris, Tiv, Idoma, Kanuri and so on in the North are lumped together as minority ethnic groups."[6]

The Nigerian conception of an ethnic minority also includes a small group of people from a different ethnic group who live in the midst of a larger ethnic group. For instance, the Ikulu people of Middle-belt Nigeria, with a population of approximately 500 000 feel that they are a minority group compared with their numerically stronger neighbours in that state like the Jabas or, even on a broader scale, when they compare themselves with the Yoruba, Igbo or the Hausa in the federation. In the same way, the Ijaw people of the Niger Delta, though numerically the fourth largest ethnic group in the country, are perceived as a minority group because they are the majority ethnic group in one state (Bayelsa) only and are a minority community in the diasporas of the six states of Rivers, Delta, Ondo, Akwa-Ibom, Cross River and Edo.

It is clear from the above description that ethnicity and tribalism in national affairs are orchestrated through the use of numbers. The current discrimination against various ethnic minorities in the Middle-belt region of Nigeria means that these ethnic groups now feel that they share a common subordinate identity. The majority also perceive them in this way and so the

---

6. Imuetinyan, Festus O. "Federalism, Ethnic Minorities and National Integration in Nigeria," in Usuanlele & Ibhawoh. *Minority Rights*, n.d. 208–209.

minority groups are liable to be subjected to political, religious, economic, educational, occupational, linguistic and other forms of discrimination.

The fear of domination then influences the way minorities react towards the majority group. Imuetinyan is right to note that "Given this fear, the political system tends to witness the manifestation of centrifugal tendencies, as each ethnic group seeks greater autonomy to protect its interests."[7]

In the name of protecting their interests, in today's Nigeria both the majority and the minority groups are striving to use the tribe as a tool to achieve their own ends, as they seek political offices and sectional control. It is fair to say that currently tribal propaganda has become a device to be used by the political elite when they campaign for one office or the other in Nigeria. This confirms what Chinua Achebe sees:

> Nothing in Nigeria's political history captures her problem of national integration more graphically than the chequered fortune of the word *tribe* [italic mine] in her vocabulary. Tribe has been accepted at one time as a friend, rejected as an enemy at another, and finally smuggled in through the backdoor as an accomplice.[8]

And now, it has sauntered through the front door of the Federal Character Commission which has institutionalised tribal affiliation. The tribe now serves as a precondition granting access to schools, employment, contract awards, revenue allocation and many other opportunities. In addition, there is another requirement, which Achebe describes as less crude but more hypocritical. Nigerians are now asked to reveal their state of origin. This informs Achebe's definition of tribalism as allowing for "discrimination against a citizen because of his place of birth"[9] or cultural affiliation. One of the consequences of this, as Achebe observes, is that

> the cult of mediocrity will bring the wheels of modernization grinding to a halt throughout the land." It could herald the demise of merit and nationalism in our political affairs. One's tribal affiliation has become the "common currency of domination, resistance, affirmation and negation.[10]

---

7.   Imuetinyan, Festus O. "Federalism, Ethnic Minorities, and National Integration in Nigeria," in *Minority Rights and the National Question in Nigeria*, 210, 211.

8.   Achebe, *Image of Africa*, 25.

9.   Achebe, *Image of Africa*, 27, 37–38.

10.   Appiah, "Mistaken Identities."

In Nigeria's political life, merit has been replaced with tribal affiliation and nationalism with religious affiliation. Achebe goes as far as to suggest that "it would be difficult to point to one important job held by the most competent person we have" because of how merit has been exchanged for tribalism."[11] In fact,

> Fear of inter-ethnic domination is a glaring political problem in Nigeria. Consequently, in analyses of Nigerian government and politics, problems of ethnicity and national integration are continuously significant and have received scholarly attention as well as public importance. Ethnic pluralism, understandably, gets reflected in the practices of governments and public policy in Nigeria.[12]

As a result, suggests Kalu, "Every Nigerian is extremely conscious of the importance of tribalism in politics." He argues that, in fact, the tribe is determining the Nigerian economy,

> This [tribal] consciousness is pervasive because administrative units, such as 'states' and local government areas, are mapped out according to tribes. Admission into institutions of learning and the distribution of national wealth are conducted by ethnic consideration."[13]

The result is that these conflicts are now institutionalized and, as Matthew Michael observes,

> The conflicting parties see any member of the opposing camp not as a human person, but as an individual expression of the institution. Thus people are often killed and even massacred, not because they committed any wrong, but because they are individual representations of the institution which the killer hates.[14]

In view of the modern practices in Nigeria, we therefore cannot define "ethnicity" to mean merely a socio-political phenomenon that is manifested in interactions between majority and minority ethnic groups within a political

---

11. Achebe, *Image of Africa*, 38.

12. Imuetinyan, Festus O. "Federalism, Ethnic Minorities, and National Integration in Nigeria," in Usuanlele & Ibhawoh. *Minority Rights*, 17.

13. Kalu, *Nigerian Condition*, 4.

14. Michael, "Liberation in Exodus," 82.

system where population, language and culture are the most prominent attributes.[15] Odukoya and Çanci point out that

> The formation of dialects within languages was one of the ways in which ethnicity – both small-scale and large-scale – became fixed in Nigeria. Although there are over 400 languages in Nigeria, only three are considered important while the rest are considered minor languages. However, the distribution of these languages is directly proportional to both political and socio-economic power, and therefore the language group to which one belongs defines his/her status in the society.[16]

Are things changing? Is the National Orientation Agency (NOA) educating the people about this issue, and is even that agency independent of political manipulation? Do its members even know their function?

---

15. Nnoli, *Ethnic Politics in Nigeria*, 94.

16. Çancı, and Odukoya "Ethnic and Religious Crises."

6

Religion: Christianity and Islam

Religion also plays a significant role in Nigerian society and is a potent force in the geopolitical development of the country. Although religion in itself is not bad, when it is manipulated by some for their personal gain it becomes dangerous and works against the national interest.

David Gooding and John Lennox lament this:

> In some parts of the world people are fighting, torturing and killing their opponents in the name of religion. And that surely shows an appalling perversion of human values; though, to be fair, it often likewise represents an equally appalling perversion of the actual tenets of the religion in whose name it is done.[1]

This potent force which was once used to unite Nigerians is now used to fan numerous conflicts in the country. Although one of the watchwords of the modern world is tolerance and religious freedom, Nigeria has been engulfed in numerous religious crises and/or conflicts between 1980 and 1994.[2] But the tension that exists between Islam and Christianity, especially in the Middle-belt region, is more complicated than just religion.

While history shows that conflict is a ubiquitous and often useful element in human relations, violent conflict is rarely productive. Nonetheless conflict, if properly diagnosed, could be the precursor to negotiation. According to Barbara A. Budjac Corvette,

> We seek to change someone's opinion because it conflicts with ours. We seek to change someone's behaviour because it conflicts with what we want. We seek to cause someone to give

---

1. Gooding and Lennox, *The Bible and Ethics*, x.
2. Çancı, and Odukoya, "Ethnic and Religious Crises," See also Warner, "Sad Rise of Boko": 38–40.

us something or do something for us because something conflicts with our ability to satisfy our need or otherwise get what we want by ourselves. Our view and analysis of conflict, therefore, directly affects negotiation approach and strategy."[3]

So how should we define 'conflict'?

Onigu Otite and Isaac Albert suggest that:

Conflicts have their objective bases in the society. The concept is validated daily over access to a variety of limited resources which are created and distributed within defined establishment and location: Conflicts are real, and serve in the above circumstances in the achievement of goal or the maintenance of claims.[4]

Meanwhile, C.M. Magagula suggests that:

Conflict is a serious disagreement, struggle, and fight arising out of differences of opinions, wishes, needs, values, and interests between and among individuals or groups.[5]

Okai cites Coser who suggests that conflict is therefore:

A struggle between and among individuals or groups over values and claims to scarce resources, status symbols, and power bases. The objective of the individuals or groups engaged in conflict is to neutralize, injure or eliminate their rivals so that they can enjoy the scarce resources, the status symbols, and power bases.[6]

In religious conflicts, it is not clear which of the above aims the antagonists want to achieve. However, R. L. Gofwen suggests that the political aims are primary. In his view, religious conflicts are a specific form of conflict between groups which vary ideologically along religious lines within a pluralistic context with each striving for political significance.[7]

Thus, while ethnic divides were of greater importance in the past, a religious divide now appears to be becoming more pronounced as religious tensions compound traditional ethnic and geopolitical rivalries, magnifying

---

3. Corvette, Barbara A. Budjac. *Conflict Management: A Practical Guide to Developing Negotiation Strategies*. Harlow: Pearson Education Ltd., 2014, 35.

4. Otite & Albert, *Community Conflicts in Nigeria*, 4.

5. Magagula, "Conflict Resolution and Management.

6. Okai, "Role of the Christian Church," 22.

7. Gofwen, *Religious Conflicts in Northern Nigeria and Nation Building: The Throes of Two Decades 1980–2000*. Cited in Nwaomah, "Religious Crises in Nigeria," 95.

underlying insecurities and grievances.[8] The past decade has seen increasing reports of sectarian violence in Nigeria's Middle Belt where these ethnic and religious communities meet. And in an ominous sign of things to come, these attacks are increasingly being framed in terms of religious and cultural conflict.

> The institutionalization of Sharia law in 12 northern states beginning in 1999 and consequent subjugation of the English legal system represented a return to Islamic primacy which has not been observed since the pre-colonial period.
>
> The inclusion under shari'a law of criminal as well as civil matters was the culmination of gradual and some would argue inevitable decline of the system of common law that was imposed on Nigeria during colonialism.[9]

The attempt to impose sharia law by force in Nigeria has been mirrored by the rise of Islamic fundamentalist movements such as the deadly Boko Haram. These authors suggest further that, as part of efforts to establish an Islamic caliphate,

> attacks on Christians and moderate Muslims by the militant group Boko Haram, which translates literally to 'Western Forbidden,' may be orchestrated with the goal of stoking religious tensions between the predominately Christian Igbo in the South and Hausa-Fulani Muslims in the North, with the Yoruba in the West representing a mix of Christianity and Islam.

Most of these conflicts

> have occurred mainly in the Middle-Belt and cultural borderline states of the Muslim north, where Muslim Hausa-Fulani groups have been pitted against non-Muslim ethnic groups in a 'dangerous convergence of religious and ethnic fears and animosities . . . [in which it] is often difficult to differentiate between religious and ethnic conflicts as the dividing line between the two is very thin.[10]

In conflicts of this nature occurring as they do along the convergence of ethnic and religious lines, it is often very difficult to tell the differences between

---

8. Zeleza, "The Causes and Costs of War in Africa: From Liberation Struggles to the 'War on Terror,'" in Zeleza (eds.) *Roots of Africa*; Marshall, *Conflict Trends in Africa,* and Siollun, *Oil, Politics and Violence,* 11–68; 97–116; 127–149.

9. Stonawski, Potančoková, Cantele & Skirbekk, "Changing religious composition," 3.

10. Osaghae & Suberu, "History of Identities."

religious and ethnic crises because the dividing line between them is "slimmer than thin."[11]

Examples of such ethno-religious conflicts are the Kafanchan-Kaduna crisis that occurred in the 1980s and 1990s, the Kaduna Sharia riots of 2000 and the Jos riots of 2001.[12] Several hundred lives were lost during the 2000 and 2001 insurrections and the crises caused violent ripple effects that spread beyond Kaduna and Jos.[13] Jan H. Boer has documented the factors that led to these conflicts very well and has suggested some solutions.[14]

Within the context of an ethnically and religiously diverse country such as Nigeria, the recent emphasis on religious identity linked to religious-specific differences could have significant political and economic implications. It is particularly important to note that

> "The emergence of militant Islamic sects and possible spread of Sharia law to additional states is potentially a response to the growing north-south gap and perceived political dominance of the South. Indeed, while its implementation has ignited hostilities particularly in the border states making up the Middle Belt, Sharia law was being applied to Muslims in most Northern states long before its formal institutionalization."[15]

Osaghae and Suberu point out that today Nigeria is faced with persistent conflicts. Nigeria has become synonymous with deep divisions which result in issues being vigorously and violently contested along intricate ethnic, religious and regional lines.[16] The issues that bring the greatest controversy are those which are regarded as essential for the existence and the validity of the state. Opposing sides tend to adopt a 'winner-takes-all' approach with regard to issues such as "the control of state power, resource allocation and citizenship".[17] Yet these solutions tend to be fragile and unstable because the people have very little in common. There is nothing to stop the forces from ripping them apart.[18]

---

11. Çancı, and Odukoya, "Ethnic and Religious Crises."

12. Osaghae and Suberu, "History of Identities," 19.

13. Enukora, "Managing Ethno-Religious Violence and Area Differentiation in Kaduna Metropolis," in Yakuba, Adegboye, Ubah &Dogo, *Crisis and conflict management in Nigeria since 1980. Vol II*, 633.

14. Boer, *Christianity and Islam; Nigeria's Decades of Blood* and *Christian: Why This Muslim*.

15. Stonawski, Potančoková, Cantele, & Skirbekk, "Changing religious composition," 4.

16. Osaghae and Suberu, "History of Identities," 4.

17. Osaghae &Suberu, 4.

18. Osaghae &Suberu, 4.

State (Politics) and Religion

Clearly, therefore, the factor that troubles our nation is the interaction between politics and religion.

It is true that, throughout history, the relationship between the state and religion has always been that of foes and allies. These two forces become allies only when there is a single dominant religion, such as was the case during the reign of Constantine in the Greco-Roman empire.[19]

It is also a fact that Africans are incurably religious. This makes it difficult to ignore the presence and role of religion in modern Nigeria. In Nigeria religion and politics

> interact in a number of important but complex ways. Whether it
> is at the local, national or international level; whether it involves
> ordinary citizens, activists or major leaders; whether it concerns
> legislative institutions, pressure groups or competing political
> parties and ideologies . . . religion and politics relate.[20]

Christianity and Islam have different views on the relationship between the state and religion. This means that in Nigeria the relationship between these two religions has usually been that of foes. As a result, inter-religion conflict regularly forms part of the dynamics of identity politics. The political elite in Nigeria have always sought to take advantage of these differences, especially during electioneering. In their quest to assume power and state resources, they constantly use patterns of political discrimination, hatred or exclusion. This perpetually changing pattern of domination breeds fears and anxieties which cause an upsurge in the struggle and intolerance.[21] In turn, this results in further conflict and instability as there is little or no sense of a unifying ideology. Because the politics of Nigeria focuses on the appeasement of religious differences, religion has attained a level of importance which means that it is difficult to challenge or overpower.

The Accra Charter on Religious Freedom and Citizenship outlines what the conference believed the African Christian approach to faith should be:

> We learn that membership in the family [of God] is consistent and
> identical with solidarity with our fellow human beings everywhere,
> that being born in relationship [with him] is a stepping stone to
> growing in relationship and maturing in responsibility. We bring

---

19. Fergusson, *Background of Early Christianity*.
20. Moyser, "Politics and Religion," 2.
21. Ibrahim & Kazah-Toure, *Ethno-Religious Identities*, 17–19, esp. p.18.

this collective understanding of ourselves into relationships in the wider society, allowing us to share in the privileges and responsibilities of membership of family and kinship, and to submit to a government of laws and regulations providing for our common security and protection. The rule of Scripture that we should care for one another is the cord of Church, society, and state (1 Cor 12:25–26).

The charter further states that,

As religious persons we are mindful of the Creator and express that by freely yielding our wills in worship of Him in the same way that we express our sense of common responsibility by banding together freely and necessarily as citizens. The moral constraints to which we are obliged to submit offer the basis for the institution of a government in which life and property are respected, evil is restrained, wrong avenged, and justice upheld so that virtue and enterprise may flourish by individual industry (Prov 8:15–17; Ps 128:2).

It ends on this note:

By the nature of the case, established freely and by common consent, government cannot do more than create the environment for good to flourish; other means are required for the production of the values essential for moral progress (Gal 5:22–23; Eph 5:9). For that purpose believers must abridge their own needs and wants and summon everyone to provide for the necessities of those less fortunate than themselves. By their example they will instill in others the duty "to do justice, to love kindness, and to walk humbly with your God" (Mic 6:8). Indeed, government that is instituted as the means of bringing us the blessings of liberty will endure only if it is answerable to the values of the rule of law, justice, equity, mercy, and moderation.[22]

There has always been tension between Christianity and Islam, however, in Nigeria this tension is heightened by the Islamic conception that westernization and democracy are informed by Christian principles (such as those mentioned in the Charter) and that westernization and democracy are therefore instruments aimed at propagating Christianity.

---

22. Accra Charter, 198.

According to Zenn and Barkindo, they regard the edifice of Western civilization as being constructed on three fundamental pillars: Western education, Judeo-Christian traditions and democracy. Shekau believes that the collaboration between these three has led to globalization and to the modern world order.[23]

In fact, these are key facets of Boko Haram's ideology. This militant Islamist sect that has been terrorizing much of Northern Nigeria since 2009 strongly opposes the provision of modern and Western education for Muslim communities. Their leader, Shekau, argues that the Western world is using Western education to infiltrate Muslim minds and destroy Islam. He therefore regards western education as the source of all that is evil in the world and believes that such systems of education must be replaced by Islamic education in which Allah is the means and the goal. Shekau argues as follows against a more comprehensive education system being implemented in the North:

> There are prominent Islamic preachers who have seen and understood that the present western style education is mixed with issues that run contrary to our beliefs in Islam. . . . We believe [rain] is a creation of god rather than an evaporation caused by the sun that condenses and becomes rain. [We do not agree that] the world is a sphere. If it runs contrary to the teachings of Allah, we reject it. We also reject the theory of Darwinism."[24]

Shekau makes it very clear that he believes that western education is the gateway to moral corruption and the decay of Muslim societies:

> Followers of western education have usurped our hearts with a philosophy and method of thinking that is contrary to the demands of Allah. They have destroyed our style of life with a system that has not been instructed to us by the Prophet of Allah. Today the government rejects the Qur'an, the Prophet of Allah and the religion of Allah in public life. It replaces these with the concept of a new world order, globalization; a new system of directing world affairs. How can you as a Muslim live in this new world order and gain paradise? This is precisely what we the

---

23. Translation of Abubakar Shekau's Tafsiri on Tawhid http://www.youtube.com/watch?feature=player_detailpage&v=vxW9Pl1rZs8)

24. Pierri and Barkindo, "Muslims in Northern Nigeria," 139.

Muslim ummah is fighting. This is what we have declared we do not want.[25]

The Christian Response

Violent conflicts and all other criminal acts are a significant indication of moral deterioration in a nation. This book would not have been necessary if the Christian response had been peaceful and had tackled the challenges positively. However, neither in the west nor in the south has the church responded well to these challenges. Joel Edwards contends that across the world the Christian church has not presented Christ credibly. He writes,

> For two thousand years the Christian church has been talking about Jesus. It has written thousands of books and preached a trillion sermons and populated countless seminars. In spite of this, the vast majority of modern Christians work with cultural misconceptions about Christ. This is due in part to poor teaching and in part to the paucity of biblical awareness about who Jesus really is . . . there is an urgent need for a biblicised church.
>
> Our Christian ignorance consequently means that people "outside" the church also have no real idea who the authentic Jesus is. We have given them an incomplete version. We have busied ourselves with conversations between ourselves, but when all is said and done, our culture knows little other than a dumbed-down Jesus.[26]

Similarly, Kreeft argues that,

> Modernist or liberal Christians in all churches and denominations essentially reduce religion to morality. This is why they specialise in morality. Christianity to them is essentially an ethic, a way of living in this world rather than a way of attaining the next. Christ becomes essentially our human teacher and example rather than God our Saviour. (He is both of course; modernist Christianity is half-Christianity, not non-Christianity.) Ethics thus becomes

---

25. Shekau, Mallam Abubakar: Nigeria, October 28, 2011, https://www.youtube.com/watch?v=eQY4GLtzLdU

26. Edwards, *Agenda for Change,* 10.

supremely important for the modernist. It is his "thing", all he has left.[27]

Orthodox Christian Response to the modern values vacuum: Conservative Protestants, both evangelical and fundamentalists, have not been able to fill the ethical needs of our time mainly because of their suspicion of the Roman Catholic acute attention to tradition, natural law, and social ethic. Broadly speaking, the Orthodox Christians are suspicious of the Roman Catholic approach because they believe that such beliefs run counter to the biblical revelation.[28]

This suggests that we cannot present Christ credibly when we are divided through conflicting worldviews. The energy that we should have used to study our sociopolitical and socioeconomic contexts so that we could empower the local churches to be God's people has been used instead to tear the church of Christ apart. What the public hears about us does not move them. They do not see an obvious demonstration of the love of Jesus Christ that can and has turned an immoral world upside down as it did initially. (Compare this with the account of the ministry of the apostles recorded in the book of Acts.) Add to this the fact that, although the Christian faith demands a holistic commitment to the person of Jesus Christ as revealed in the Scriptures, today the Christian community is busy pursuing the same things as the unbelieving society: the gods and goddesses of the religion of Mammon – wealth, power and democracy. What is valued in the political culture of our society is also valued in the different Christian denominations. No wonder, Achebe says: "This house has fallen."

---

27. Kreeft, *Back to Virtue*, 21–22, 25

28. Kreeft, *Back to Virtue*, 21–22, 25

Section Three

Seeking Solutions

When moral failures are not corrected, they can easily be passed on to the next generation both directly and indirectly. In order to prevent this we must seek knowledge as we know that without knowledge we cannot discover how to live so that all people may flourish. This is why we send our children to school. Peter Kreeft has pointed out that the Greek philosopher, Aristotle, taught that

> there are three reasons for seeking knowledge. The most important one is truth, the next is moral action, and least important is power, or the ability to make things: technique, technology, know-how. [1]

Today, however, at school one is mainly taught how to pursue power. In our modern world where democracy is idolized, power has extraordinary value. The quest for political, economic and social power has distorted the practice of morality and has replaced truth-telling. It has even impacted our outlook as Christians. Nigerian Christians have been so overwhelmed by the need to have power that they hardly remember that in the Bible God says, "Not by might, nor by power, but by my Spirit" (Zech 4:6). When we act morally, we are better than our philosophy, while our ancestors were worse than theirs.

---

1. Kreeft, *Back to Virtue*, 21–22, 25.

7

Attempts by Government

Nigeria's various administrations have made several attempts to tackle the many moral issues in the country by instilling desirable social values and attitudes into our citizens. Such efforts, however, seem to have yielded little or no result as people are still deeply involved in moral misconduct on a daily basis. Nonetheless, we should note what the administrations have tried.

The Shehu Shagari Administration (1979–1983) introduced the Ethical Revolution;[1] the Buhari – Idiagbon Administration (1984–1985) introduced the War Against Indiscipline (WAI); the Babangida Administration (1985–1993) introduced Mass Mobilization for Self-Reliance, Social Justice and Economic Recovery (MAMSER) and the Abacha Administration (1993–1998) (re)introduced the ideas of the War Against Indiscipline and launched the War Against Indiscipline and Corruption (WAIC). Then the Obasanjo Administration (1999–2007) introduced both the Independent Corrupt Practices and other Related Offences Commission (ICPC) and the Economic and Financial Crimes Commission (EFCC). The National Orientation Agency (NOA) was also established in order to curb all forms of antisocial behaviours through value re-orientation programmes.[2] Other educational and social programmes and commissions were also inaugurated in the same effort. This brought the Change Programme, National Youth Service Corps, Unity Schools and Federal Character Commission into being.

Since these government attempts are not really the focus of this book, I have chosen to analyse only one as it is germane to this topic: Shagari's Ethical Revolution. I shall then look briefly at other related programmes, such as the National Orientation Agency, the National Youth Service Corps and the Unity Schools.

---

1. Oji, *Nigerian Ethical Revolution; and* Oji, *Action Phase* .
2. Adedigba & Wahab, "Degenerated Moral Values," 50.

Shagari's Goal for Nigeria

The idea of an 'Ethical Revolution' arose because it was felt that Nigeria had lost all hope of restoring its moral standards. When the idea was introduced, however, it was "ridiculed with disarming scepticism" because the nation was so deeply immersed "in ethical decay and indiscipline."[3]

He declared that the Ethical Revolution must not be merely a "cosmetic dress-up effort, a temporary palliative remedy, nor a makeshift change rooted adventitiously in the hopes for quick results." It must also not be mere "utopia-seeking" but that the country's frustration should inspire hope for human flourishing or a future with hope. Oji urged that the ethical revolution should be:

> well planned and backed by a deliberate national consensus that unleashes an irreversible movement; a movement which will transcend parties and administrations above a truly worthy legacy to be left by the present generation, and which will in time gather enough momentum and effective motive force to land this nation by the turn of the century upon the solid and respectable platform of world leadership, internal order and stable prosperity. It is conceived to be a programme for a non-violent, self-corrective Ethical Revolution, such as the world has never seen before.[4]

Oji also said that a revolution like this must aim at,

> creating in the long run a powerful distinguishing national ethical culture for Nigeria, which will exemplify the impact of our strong religious tradition and be a mitigating influence on the onslaught we face from disruptive foreign cultural influence in this age of rapid global interaction.[5]

Thus the Ethical Revolution in Nigeria was

> meant to produce in us deliberately a fundamental change of a long-term decisive impact, to move this nation steadily and permanently in [a] discernible new direction.[6]

This new direction must be one of

---

3. Oji, *Nigerian Ethical Revolution*, 11.
4. See also, Achebe, *Image of Africa*, 29.
5. Oji, *Action Phase*, 35–36.
6. Oji, *Nigerian Ethical Revolution*, 17.

self-reliance and dedication to excellence in leadership, in discipline, in orderliness, in hard work, in honesty, in morality, in mutual respect and tolerance, along with the submission of our citizenry to God in national affairs and personal pursuits.[7]

A campaign of twenty years was envisaged. During this time it was hoped that the idea of an ethical transformation would realign all the facets of the nation. In August 1979 General Olusegun Obasanjo was so sure that the initiative would be successful that he predicted that "Nigeria will become one of the ten leading nations in the world by the end of the century."[8]

However the revolution, despite all the efforts of those who carried this vision, failed to influence the nation to transcend the ties of parties, administrations, tribes and religion.

General Obasanjo's prediction did not come true. The failure of the nation to see the seriousness of the moral emergency has meant that Nigeria does not occupy a position of power or leverage today.

But this failure also affected the situation within the country. The lack of ethical behaviour means that the country continues to lack "internal order and stable prosperity."[9] The failure of the initiative means that the country still lacks transformative and forward-thinking leaders. As a result, Nigeria now desperately needs

some drastic social clean-up effort but only under a leader who himself can set impeccable example for the nation to follow in pursuing such a drive as peaceful, orderly programme of change.[10]

Nigeria's lack of transformative leadership has been pointed out again and again and cannot be overemphasized. Achebe is on record as saying, "The trouble with Nigeria is simply and squarely a failure of leadership," and that "Nigerians are what they are only because their leaders are not what they should

---

7. Oji, *Nigerian Ethical Revolution,* 17.

8. Oji, *Nigerian Ethical Revolution,* 17.

9. See Oji, *Nigerian Ethical Revolution; Kalu, Nigerian Condition;* Achebe, *Image of Africa;* Ijatuyi-Morphé, *Africa's Social and Religious;* Agang, *Impact of Ethnic;* Ngozi Okonjo-Iweala, *Reforming the Unreformable;* Zeleza, "Causes and Costs The Causes and Costs of War in Africa: From Liberation Struggles to the 'War on Terror,'" in Zeleza (eds.) *Roots of Africa;* Marshall, *Conflict Trends in Africa* and Siollun, *Oil, Politics and Violence.*

10. Oji, *The Nigerian Ethical Revolution,* 119.

be."[11] Many Nigerians share the opinion that "the only factor standing between Nigeria and greatness is leadership."[12] Achebe elaborates further, asserting that

> There is nothing basically wrong with the Nigerian character. There is nothing wrong with the Nigerian land or climate or water or air or anything else. The Nigerian problem is the unwillingness or inability of its leaders to rise to the responsibility, to the challenge of personal example which are the hallmarks of true leadership.[13]

Like Achebe, Oji concludes that what is needed in Nigeria "is not a theoretical discourse at a seminar, nor frequent charismatic orations on a soapbox." It needs "the highest possible measures of ethical dedication and discipline for their satisfactory accomplishment."[14] Our problem in Nigeria is the erosion of moral character. The failure of the leaders is the failure of the larger society. The home, the church, the mosque and all our other social systems and institutions have not produced moral leaders.

The Ethical Revolution was not able to address our moral disorder. Neither have the various other attempts by the different administrations in government. Despite the sentiments expressed in our national anthem and our pledge, Nigeria is morally bankrupt.

NOA—National Orientation Agency

In 2005 the administration established this agency, commissioning it:

> To consistently raise awareness, provide timely and credible feedback; positively change attitudes, values and behaviours; accurately and adequately inform; and sufficiently mobilize citizens to act in ways that promote peace, harmony; and national development.[15]

One of this agency's many functions is the "Enlightenment of the general public on Government policies, programmes and activities." However, we have to wonder if the agency has indeed informed citizens of their responsibilities.

Can we even claim that it has created sufficient awareness of the government's reasons for its decisions? The answer seems to be that it has

---

11. Achebe, *Image of Africa*, 22, 31.
12. Mohammed & Ayeni, "Political Leadership in Nigeria," 321.
13. Achebe, *Image of Africa*, 22. See also: Lee, *From Third World*, 356.
14. Oji, *Nigerian Ethical Revolution*, 126.
15. National Orientation Agency, "About Us,"

not. This lack of information led to the birth of movements such as Occupy Nigeria, which began on Monday 2 January 2012. All over the country as well as among the diaspora in London, citizens protested about the rise in fuel costs, participating in acts of civil disobedience such as strikes and demonstrations, even though many of them did not know what a 'fuel subsidy' was, let alone what impact it would have on their lives.[16] The government had done nothing to inform its citizens adequately about what was happening. The protests, however, provoked a response from the government as it hastened to introduce the Subsidy Reinvestment and Empowerment Programme (SURE-P).[17]

However, if the governments of the day do not learn to inform the nation about the reasons behind their policies, the NOA will not be able:

> To develop a Nigerian society that is orderly, responsible and disciplined, where citizens demonstrate core values of honesty, hard work and patriotism; where democratic principles and ideals are upheld; and where peace and social harmony reign.

Nor will it be able to

> Awaken the consciousness of Nigerians to their responsibilities to the promotion of national unity, citizens' commitment to their human rights to build a free, just and progressive society; [or to] develop among Nigerians of all ages and sex, social and cultural values and awareness which will inculcate the spirit of patriotism, nationalism, self-discipline and self-reliance.[18]

Federal Character Commission

Another attempt by the government to ease ethnic and religious tensions in Nigeria was the establishment of the Federal Character Commission (FCC). FCC is one of fourteen Federal Executive bodies and was established by Act No 34 of 1996 to "implement and enforce the principles of fairness and equity" in the distribution of public posts and socio-economic infrastructures among

---

16. See News Agencies such as the Guardian, France24: https://www.theguardian.com/world/2012/jan/16/nigeria-restores-fuel-subsidy-protests. See also Akinbobola, "Bid to End Subsidy"; Monica Mark, (8 January 2012). "Nigeria Faces Mass Strike and Protests Over Discontinued State Fuel Subsidy."

17. See "Nigeria Subsidy Reinvestment and Empowerment Programme (SURE-P): Maternal and Child Health Initiative," https://www.worldbank.org/en/programs/sief-trust-fund/brief/nigeria-subsidy-reinvestment-and-empowerment-programme-sure-p

18. National Orientation Agency, "About Us."

the various federating units of the Federal Republic of Nigeria.[19] Although not many Nigerians would agree that it has achieved its aims, the goal of ensuring fairness and equity is a good one.

One of the functions of the commission is formulated as follows:

> to work out an equitable formula, subject to the approval of the President, for the distribution of all cadres of posts in the civil and public service of the Federation and of the State, the armed forces, the Nigerian Police Force and other security agencies, bodies corporate owned by the federal or a State Government and Extra-Ministerial Departments and parastatals of the Federation and States.

However, the distribution of power since 2015 has raised a great deal of concern. One of two scenarios must be true. Either the President, who reserves the right to agree and disagree with the recommendation of the commission, has not implemented the commission's recommendations or its formulae for distribution are flawed. What is certain is that it has failed "to promote, monitor and enforce compliance with the principles of proportional sharing of all bureaucratic, economic, media and political posts at all levels of government."[20] It is not true that each state is equitably represented in all national institutions and in public enterprises, nor is it true that the best person is appointed to each position. Although the commission has the right to take legal action against any organ of the state that fails to comply, clearly this does not happen.

And there is a further problem when quotas are introduced. In the years just after independence (1970s to 1980s), Nigeria built on what it had inherited and developed one of the best merit-based civil services in Africa. In those early years, Nigerian citizens were hired as consultants to assist other African countries in establishing their government departments, police forces and civil services. However, as a result of our decades of martial law, the civil service is no longer merit-based but representative-based, regardless of quality. Ngozi Okonjo-Iweala, Nigeria's Coordinating Minister for the Economy and Minister of Finance from 2007–2011, documented her experiences, showing how tribal sentiments, sectional interests and religious bigotry have eaten deep into the Nigerian public service and undermined the Federal Character Commission.

---

19. Federal Character Commission., http://www.federalcharacter.gov.ng/index.php/about-us. See also Joshua, Loromeke and Olanrewaju, "Quota System", 1–10.

20. Federal Character Commission, "Guiding Principles," https://federalcharacter.gov.ng/1189-2/

Despite several attempts by government to reform the system, it is difficult to point to a political position in the country that is held by the most qualified person. The Federal Character Principle has replaced merit with mediocrity and has sacrificed merit for ethnic, religious and sectional representation that often undermines excellence and replaces it with even more mediocrity or representation. These appointments boost the ethnic or religious group but do not allow the nation to progress. To address this problem the Federal Character Principle needs to be restructured.

Nigeria's failure to deliver quality services, particularly in the areas of education, health, transportation, environment, works, finance, communication and power has several severe implications. For example, Okonjo-Iweala also notes that

> The skills gap in the civil service was important. To my consternation, I found out after an internal census of the Ministry of Finance that I ordered as part of the reform process that the bulk of my ministry staff—70 percent—were lower-level administrative staff, clerks, and cleaners with only high school education or the equivalent. Only 13 percent were graduates of universities or other tertiary institutions, and just 8 percent had degrees related to accounting or economics. Overall, the government estimated that about 70 percent of federal civil servants had no more than a high school diploma, with less than 5 percent possessing modern computer skills. Clearly such a workforce was not equipped to deliver our ambitious development program.[21]

This skills gap at all levels in the civil service is yet to be addressed by the Nigerian government. However, the Nigerian government does not even know the size of its workforce! Okonjo-Iweala acknowledges that,

> No one quite knew the exact size of the civil service at federal or state levels. At the time of the reform, in 2004, estimates for the core federal civil service ranged from 141,440 from the Federal Civil Service Commission to 160,000 from the Office of the Head of the Civil Service . . . If extra ministerial government departments and state enterprises were added, then these estimates rose to about 1 million. Adding the states brought the number up to an estimated 2.3 million public servants.[22]

---

21. Okonjo-Iweala, *Reforming the Unreformable*, 52
22. Okonjo-Iweala, *Reforming the Unreformable*, 52–53.

This lack of a comprehensive census, together with poor administration and an inadequate personnel control system, has led to several problems. There is a constant cry from all over the country that 'ghost workers' and 'ghost pensioners' are benefitting financially. The solution of allowing every governor or minister to have a database specific to the state or ministry in which that minister administers is deeply flawed. Nigeria's databases are now as numerous as its political parties and former governors!

School Related Programmes: Exchange Programme, NYSC and Unity School

The government has also tried to promote national unity by establishing various education-related agencies to enhance the integration programme of Nigeria. Among them is the National Youth Services Corps Scheme, which was created in a bid to reconstruct and reconcile the country after the Nigerian Civil war. The decree by which it was established declares that it was being formed "with a view to the proper encouragement and development of common ties among the youths of Nigeria and the promotion of national unity."[23]

The Corps set out to inculcate

> discipline in Nigerian youths by instilling in them a tradition of industry at work, and of patriotic and loyal service to Nigeria in any situation they may find themselves, [and] to raise the moral tone of the Nigerian youths by giving them the opportunity to learn about higher ideals of national achievement, social and cultural improvement; to develop in the Nigerian youths the attitudes of mind, acquired through shared experience and suitable training which will make them more amenable to mobilisation in the national interest; to develop common ties among the Nigerian youths and promote national unity and integration; to remove prejudices, eliminate ignorance and confirm at first hand the many similarities among Nigerians of all ethnic groups."[24]

Although, the NYSC has done remarkably well in its attempt to live up to the country's expectations, consistency seems to be a major problem.

---

23. NYSC, https://www.nysc.gov.ng/aboutscheme.html see "About the Scheme"
24. NYSC, https://www.nysc.gov.ng/objectives.html see "Objectives of the Scheme"

As we have considered the various attempts of the federal government to inculcate good moral values among its citizens, it should have become clear that unity in the nation can only be achieved if we are prepared to accept that our group interests must be brought into harmony with those of the nation at all levels. Group interests (religious or ethnic) are legitimate and should be satisfied. However attempts to satisfy every ethnic and religious desire will only lead to dissatisfaction.

8

Taking a Stand

The last chapter shows that, despite the attempts of various governments to stem the flow, morality in Nigeria continues to decline. The moral deterioration is occurring slowly but steadily. It does not happen overnight!

Neither is Nigeria the only area in the world where this is happening. Humanity, Mark Walters suggests, has moved from the stage when biblical morality was 'trendy' to 'non-biblical morality', then on to 'immorality' and lastly to the present time which he describes as 'amorality'.

> In 1800–1900s, people believed that there was such a thing as right and wrong and that certain things were wrong, and they could tell why. 1900–1950s, most people couldn't tell why. 1960-early 1970s, not many people cared. Late 1970-present, there is no such thing as right or wrong![1]

Josh McDowell echoes this, saying that,

> Formerly, most people's concept of morality was derived from an external standard – what God said in Scripture. But in our post-Christian society, most people's concept of morality is based on their own feelings and opinions. This opens the door to morality without standards.[2]

The fact that our moral values have deteriorated in Nigeria means that we have to grapple with issues such as drug abuse, promiscuity, dysfunctional families, assassination and murder, as well as political instability. In a study on why Nigeria needs to base itself on a set of values, Donatus Njoku adds to

---

1. Mark Water, *Moral Choices: Tough Questions, Clear Answers Made Simple*, Tennessee: AMG Publishers, 2002, 4–5

2. Josh McDowell, *How to Help Your Child say No to Sexual Pressure* (Kaduna: Evangel Publishers Ltd., 1987), 30.

this list, pointing out that, if moral values are disregarded, this can result in the pursuit of wealth without knowledge or character, pleasure without conscience, commerce without morality, worship without sacrifice, science without humanity and politics without principles.[3] In other words, when the value system of a nation crumbles, the disciplines and practices that should lead to development and stability are disregarded and fade into the shadows. Recently on Radio Nigeria, the commentator made the following sad observation about the decline in morality in present-day Nigeria,

> The crisis of the value system in Nigeria suggests that the growth and progress of the society is being retarded in many aspects through materialistic tendencies. Materialism has taken over government and political institutions in the country. It has also invaded traditional and cultural institutions, while the religious places seem to be more materialistic than the secular society. The malady of value crisis has predicated Nigeria as an open society in which anything goes. There is high level of distrust and suspicion to the extent that everybody has become a suspect of misplaced value. Immorality and lack of sanctity of life have continued to increase as suicide, banditry, murder and kidnapping have become daily occurrence that pervaded the society. One thing remains sacrosanct, the dominant traits in the character of Nigerians should remain the overriding values of the people and the nation. Nigerians must therefore return to the era where they extolled good values; they must become a people with genuine love for one another and stop the killing of fellow Nigerians at the slightest provocation. Nigeria should become a nation where Nigerians can accommodate and accept one another's beliefs, culture and general way of life.[4]

Identifying and discussing the vices that reflect the deterioration of moral values publically has become usual among concerned Nigerians. Many of them paint rosy pictures about 'the good old days' when good values were extolled in Nigeria. Joseph E. Harris, for example, looks back longingly to the era when Nigeria received impressive international exposure; to the time when Nigerian spokesmen commanded world attention; to the time when. Nigeria denounced

---

3. Donatus I. Njoku, "Re-Orientation of Value System in Nigeria: A Critic" *Global Journal of Arts, Humanities and Social Sciences, Vol.3, No. 11,* November, (2015), 25–32.

4. Nehemiah Anini, "Value Reorientation for the Nation's Development" Radio Nigeria (January 27, 2020).

the corruption of Ghana's Jerry Rawlings, and the acts of revenge taken by Liberia's Sergeant Doe against the Tolbert regime; to the time when Nigeria criticized Tanzania's invasion of Uganda in order to help overthrow Amin.[5] While it is appropriate to use such information to admonish Nigerians and to urge us to return to our former values, the big question of how we are to do so remains unanswered.

True, actions such as the inclusion of Civic Education as a subject in the Nigerian Junior and Secondary School curriculum may provide a ray of hope, especially if the curriculum makes children aware of the negative ideologies which are plaguing the Nigerian society. This may influence younger Nigerians to cultivate socially acceptable norms and moral values that promote and establish nationhood.

However the education curriculum alone is not enough. We also need to ensure that the voices of concerned Nigerians in key leadership positions echo in all the nooks and crannies of our country. For example, our people should be encouraged to listen to leaders like the Catholic Bishop of the Sokoto Diocese, Matthew Kukah. Speaking recently at the burial of a seminarian who had been killed by kidnappers in Kaduna, he called the Nigerian government under President Buhari to order. In a speech that went viral throughout the country, he challenged the Nigerian leadership:

> The president has displayed the greatest degree of insensitivity in managing our country's rich diversity. He has subordinated the larger interests of the country to the hegemonic interests of his co-religionists and clansmen and women. Today, our years of hypocrisy, duplicity, fabricated integrity, false piety, empty morality, fraud and Pharisaism have caught up with us. Nigeria is on the crossroads and its future hangs precariously in a balance. This is a wakeup call for us. Nigeria is at a point where we must call for a verdict. There must be something that a man, nay, a nation should be ready to die for. Sadly, or even tragically, today, Nigeria does not possess that set of goals or values for which any sane citizen is prepared to die for her.[6]

Perhaps, the multiplication of such voices will inspire concerned citizens and Nigerian leaders to be truly proactive and not simply to make empty

---

5. Joseph E. Harris, *Africans and Their History*, New York: Penguin Group, 1987, 252.

6. John Shiklam, "Kukah Accuses Buhari of insensitivity in Managing Nigeria's Diversity", in *ThisDay Newspaper (online)*. https://www.thisdaylive.com/index.php/2020/02/12/kukah-accuses-buhari-of-insensitivity-in-managing-nigerias-diversity/

comments when the blood of the innocent is spilled. Nigerians must decide as a matter of principle to give peace a chance. Our former President, Goodluck Jonathan, set an example when he publicly declared that his political ambition was not worth the blood of any Nigerian. When he declared his candidacy in the presidential race at Eagle Square, Abuja, he said:

> I have come to preach love, not hate. I have come to break you away from divisive tendencies of the past which has slowed down our drive to nationhood. I have no enemies to fight. You are my friends and we share a common destiny.[7]

The former president regards himself as a fulfilled man because he chose the interests of his country ahead of his personal interests. Sadly there are few African leaders who have the moral courage to emulate him. Yet the need to embrace peace is indeed one of the key strategies that will help us to overcome the divisions and conflicts of the past which have slowed our drive toward nationhood and have robbed us of our ability to develop national moral values.

The Christian community can go further. It can help to encourage the conversation about nation-building by upholding and promoting moral values from a biblical perspective. The attention of our Christian citizens needs to be drawn to the fact that the moral values in the national anthem and pledge echo the truths expressed in the Holy Bible. The Bible also proclaims the need for love, truth, justice and unity.

However, in our postmodern world, the meanings of these words have been distorted so that they can mean different things in different contexts. It is important therefore that we clarify them so that we can see what Nigerians will be thinking when they hear them.[8]

Love

Perhaps nowadays we think of love as some 'mushy' vague emotion. The ancient Greeks realized that it was such a vast concept that they used eight different words to explain it. A number of these ideas are reflected in our anthem and pledge.

---

7. Goodluck Ebele Jonathan, *My Transition Hours*. Kingwood, Texas: Ezekiel Books, 2018, 11.

8. *The Westminster Dictionary of Theological Terms*, 2nd ed., s.v.

(1) "Eros" or Erotic Love

Although this passionate and intense love generally refers to sexual desires, the word can also be used to describe a love of materialism or violence. This type of love can possess or enslave people so that they lose their self-control and do not hesitate to oppress, exploit and dehumanize others [9] (see Song 8:6–7). This grabbing love is not the kind of love the anthem is referring to.

(2) "Philia" or Affectionate Love

This is a type of love that is felt among friends who have endured hard times together. It therefore refers to the kind of devoted friendship that we who fought for our freedom together can share. It suggests the fellowship that younger citizens can share if they serve our country together.

(3) "Storge" or Familiar Love

'Storge' refers primarily to the love which is known as kinship. As we see in Nigeria, it can be both a blessing and an obstacle to our progress. One's family background can prevent one from seeing things through the eyes of others.

(4) "Ludus" or Playful Love

The Greeks thought of this as a playful form of love. It covers the kind of feelings we have in the early stages of falling in love: the fluttering heart, the flirting and teasing, and the feelings of euphoria. This aspect of love is referred to in 'pop music' but not in our national anthem.

(5) "Mania" or Obsessive Love

'Mania' refers to a possessive or jealous love which leads people to consider love purely for what they get out of it. Such people are motivated by the need to feel good about themselves. I suspect we can all point to people in our communities who love like this, but this is not the love our anthem proposes.

---

9. *The New International Dictionary; New Testament Theology, Vol 2,*s.v.

(6) "Pragma" or Enduring Love

Pragma suggests a love that has aged and matured. It describes the love between people who have learned to make compromises and who have learnt patience and tolerance. One's love for one's country must also mature like this.

(7) "Philautia" or Self Love

This is not referring to the unhealthy vanity or self-obsession that is focused on achieving personal fame or fortune. Instead it focuses on the fact that, if we do not love ourselves, we cannot love others for we cannot share something we do not have. This love reminds us that, when we have the strength to love ourselves, our tribes and affiliates, then we will be able to share our love with others.

(8) "Agape" or Selfless Love

This is the highest and most radical type of love. The word 'agape' refers to "strong feelings of personal affection, care, and desire for the well-being of others," despite their flaws and shortcomings. Agape is also known as 'spiritual love.' Christians recognize that this kind of love is one of God's primary characteristics (1 John 4:8; 16).

As humans created in God's image, we are His image bearers here on earth. This means that we should be demonstrating this kind of love to our country, our fellow citizens and to our world (1 Cor 13:1–13, Gal 5:14, 22–23; Eph 5:2; 1 John 4:7–21). It is unconditional love, bigger than ourselves, showing boundless compassion and an infinite empathy, giving ourselves to those in need of mercy and compassion. It is therefore the purest form of love and is free from desires and expectations.

As Peter Kreeft explains,

> Agape is what is meant, of course—that new, specific, radical kind of love that the world simply had not seen before Christ—not natural, human love.[10]

He goes on to remind us that it was his agape love that brought Jesus Christ to the planet

> to suffer Hell on the Cross to save us rebels, the love that kissed the traitor Judas, suffered the soldier's slaps and sneers, and prayed,

---

10. Kreeft, *Back to Virtue*, 76.

"Father, forgiven them, for they know not what they do." Was that love ever seen before Christ? Could that love ever be confused with ordinary, humanly-attainable, natural love? [11]

The self-love which Christ's love encourages is not the opposite of agape love:

> The wise Greeks, however, noticed that [self-love] came in two forms. There was a negative kind of self-love, which was a selfish hunger to gain personal pleasures, money and public honours,
>
> . . .
>
> Luckily Aristotle had spotted a more positive version of self-love, one that enhanced our wider capacity to love. "All friendly feelings for others," he wrote, "are extensions of a man's feelings for himself." The message was that when you like yourself and feel secure in yourself, then you will have plenty of love to give. Similarly, if you know what makes you happy, then you will be in a stronger position to find a way of extending that happiness to those around you. If, on the other hand, you are uncomfortable with who you are, or harbour some self-loathing, then you will have little love to offer others. [12]

The distinction Kreeft highlights is important if we wish to live as God instructed us, loving our neighbours in Nigeria.

Truth

While love is the greatest character virtue, truth is another of the moral virtues referred to in our national anthem – a virtue which is often disregarded in our modern or postmodern world.

Like love, truth has a number of nuances. For example, the Old Testament uses the word in two senses. The word can refer to the intellectual, cognitive or factual issues which people can ascertain to be true or false (see Deut 17:4, 1 Kg 10:6). But it can also refer to moral truth and be a description of one who is dependable, consistent and reliable. This reliability is one of the attributes of God (Ps 31:5, 103:4; Jer 10:10).

In the New Testament, the word refers first to the dependability, truthfulness and uprightness of character that is approved by God and by

---

11. Kreeft, *Back to Virtue*, 76.
12. Krznaric, *How Should We Live*, 10

other people. Second it refers to truth as being complete in and of itself. Third, the word suggests something that is more than a mere appearance or shadow or copy. It is real.[13] From this we realize that truth is a primary aspect of God's character. That is why Jesus is also described as the 'Truth.' Jesus assures his disciples (throughout all the ages) that they will know truth in all its fullness if they continue in his promises. This truth will set them free.

Philip E. Dow argues that a passion for truth is marked by intellectual courage, intellectual carefulness, intellectual fair-mindedness, intellectual curiosity, intellectual tenacity, intellectual honesty and intellectual humility.[14] We need to cultivate and nurture such a passion for truth and its consequent virtues in Nigeria.

Justice

The Latin word 'justus' means 'uprightness.' Classically this meant that each person should receive what is due to him or her. However, as Ronald Sider has noted, "Justice is easier to demand than to define."[15]

The problem lies in the fact that one cannot define justice without grasping that it is rooted in God. God is just, and he expects humans whom he has created in his image and likeness to be just. Human laws and justice should therefore reflect his divine laws and should be designed to achieve his desires and expectations. Biblically, 'justice' emphasizes right relationships and focuses on people receiving a fair share of the God-given resources in society. Though human laws and justice may not be perfect, they should not in any way "invalidate the claim that human attempts at just laws ought to be grounded in the divine standard of justice."[16]

Society's use of the word 'justice' shows us the huge responsibility that being just places on our shoulders. We talk about 'procedural justice' which means that our courts should judge cases fairly. Then there is 'distributive justice' that speaks to the fact that the goods of society (land, wealth, education and so on) are or should be distributed fairly. Third, we talk of 'retributive justice' when one receives what is due as a result of what one has done. (This usually refers to punishment for evil actions.). Finally, there is 'social justice' which means that everyone has both rights and obligations in a society. This implies being

---

13. *New Bible Dictionary*, s.v. "truth".

14. Dow, *Virtuous Minds*, 24, 28–75.

15. Sider, *Just Politics*, 77.

16. Sider, 77

able to participate in the institutions and processes of the society. Social justice can only exist when all the previous aspects of justice are present.[17]

God's righteousness is clearly intrinsic to all aspects of justice. Justice therefore is an attribute that emanates from the hearts of those who fear and love God (Lk 18:2, 6). This places the burden on Christians. We are the ones who should be setting the tone in our society. We must begin with righteous living and good neighbourliness (1 Thess 2:10). This implies giving preferential treatment to the vulnerable member(s) of society and creating social structures that can provide the checks and balances so that the economic, social and political power is not used to disadvantage the poor. A society that denies justice to the poor, to orphans, to foreigners and indeed to the needy is a cursed society (see Deut 19).

The biblical narrative of justice reveals that kings, political and religious leaders are to lead the nation in seeking justice, nevertheless, all humans are expected "to act justly and to love mercy and to walk humbly with [their] God" (Mic 6:8). Justice, therefore, is related to love and grace and truth.

J. I. Packer sums up what we have said: "Justice means straightness in a physical sense, conformity to acceptable standards of moral values and to that which God wills, or to those activities which result from it" (Rev 15:3).[18]

Yet corruption, even in the judiciary, has left those who need justice at the mercy of their exploiters and oppressors. And sometimes, even laws that are justly enforced in a region can limit its economic, social, spiritual and political development because they are not founded on God's ideals.

Unity

This is the fourth moral virtue which is mentioned in our anthem. Etymologists tell us that the word 'unity' came into use at the end of the thirteenth century and that it refers to the "state or property of being one." The word therefore can imply various kinds of 'oneness': intellectual, emotional, spiritual and sexual. In each case it refers to a mutually consensual relationship built on trust and truth-telling. People develop feelings of trust and emotional or physical closeness. Of course, feelings can change so there is a need to continue to work at the process.

Note however that although unified people come together to achieve a purpose, they remain distinct. Thus there is unity in diversity. This is important

---

17. Sider, 77.
18. *New Bible Dictionary*, s.v. "justice".

as it means that one can embrace even those who are different and those who tend to exclude others. This is an important part of Christian discipleship and coaching. We cannot have an impact on someone else's life if we are not prepared to get to know them or to permit them to know us closely.

Despite what we sing in our national anthem, these four concepts are largely ignored, whereas they should preoccupy all patriots who are in search of permanent peace and stability in Nigeria. Without these values of love, truth-telling, justice and unity, the agents of change in our systems cannot function.

9

The Challenges We Face

It is often said that 'when Nigeria coughs the whole African continent catches a cold.' Nigeria is said to be the most populous and influential black nation on the continent. In fact there is no major country where Nigerians are not found in sizeable numbers. Millions of Nigerians live in and contribute to other countries around the world as they seek to escape economic instability. It follows therefore that, if anything affects Nigeria's moral and ethical values, the global community's perception of Nigerians will be badly affected.

But we find ourselves torn apart. Nigeria has emerged from a tradition which accepted that the good of the group was paramount in the modern world of choices. Jurgen Moltmann, the German theologian, describes the modern world as follows:

> In modern societies, the values of personal liberty are paramount, placed higher than the values of sociality, of belonging to a certain group. Life is no longer moulded by tradition. We live in free-choice societies because we believe that a society can only be creative in the individual persons that constitute it. Consequently, with us, nothing must be accepted as predetermined and decreed. Everyone must be able to decide everything for himself or herself: free choice of school, free choice of job or profession, free choice of a partner, where a choice of where to live, free political choice, free choice of religion, and so on. We are even working on the possibility of being able to decide our genetic make-up for ourselves. Nothing must be "just fate", not even a person's gender. We must be able to determine everything ourselves.[1]

---

1. Moltmann, *God for a Secular Society*, 85.

Many Nigerians now find themselves dangling in mid-air somewhere between the individualism of the West and the communal tradition of Africa. On the one hand, there are those who no longer believe that anyone has the right to tell them what is true. In fact, they do not even believe that there is an absolute truth for they regard all truth as relative. However, on the other hand, there are those who still believe that there are traditional absolutes which include, among other things, the truth.

Miguel E. Banasez, a Mexican scholar and social critic, notes that cultural change is responsible for the present ethical and moral predicament in which humanity finds itself. He admits that it is natural for cultures to change slowly all the time, as they adjust to new circumstances and to the ideas of the younger generations. But he goes on to argue that this change can be either 'virtuous' or 'vicious', depending on the decisions made in response to those circumstances.

Banasez lists six agents of cultural change that militate against private and public moral integrity: family, school, religion, media, leadership and law. Although his study was not conducted in Nigeria, it is nonetheless useful for us to note his findings. He concludes that:

> The monopoly that families held on the dissemination of values for millennia was transformed by the appearance of organised religion starting in the eighth century BC. The resulting family–church duopoly reigned for centuries, until the expansion of education and of public schooling during the industrial revolution narrowed the scope of the church's influence. In addition, exchanges of opinion within groups (which would eventually become media), structures years of leadership, and systems of rules (which would evolve into laws) allowed societies to adapt ideas and structures to suit changing conditions. The power of the media to transmit values was boosted by the introduction of the printing press in the 15th century, and later by the advent of the movies (1896), radio (1909), television (1948), the Internet (1992), and now social media (2004), outcompeting with families, schools, and churches on value dissemination to children and youth. The impact of leadership and the law on children and youth, however, is remote and indirect, because it runs mainly through adults and institutions.[2]

---

2. Basanez E., Miguel, *A World of Three Cultures: Honor, Achievement and Joy* (Oxford: Oxford University Press, 2016), 158.

The cultural changes in Nigeria are enormous. In order to get back on track, we need a humanising moral education to encourage our citizens to adopt an inclusive lifestyle, taking into consideration not just their own personal needs or those of their specific group, but also the needs and aspirations of their fellow citizens.

However if such education looked at the moral issues in our country only from a human point of view, the Nigerian conundrum would be insurmountable. It is only when we see things from God's perspective that we are able to see that there is hope for Nigeria. Contrary to what many believe Nigeria is not merely a 'geographical expression' or 'a marriage of convenience'. Nigeria is God's idea, and Nigeria is therefore God's nation.

It is a sad truth, however, that the values which God entrusted to us – love, truth, justice and unity – have been discarded. The fact that love, truth, justice and unity are hardly visible in our country signifies that there is indeed a worrisome rapid decline in our ethical and moral values. Here, as in many other countries across the globe, people are trading their moral and ethical values for material and monetary rewards. Modern men and women have decided to replace them with another value: money. Sadly, many young Nigerians now assume that honour and joy can be attained without any such standards.

Truth is also being short-changed. On the TV programme, 'Good Morning Nigeria' (NTA, May 18, 2020) one of Nigeria's great minds said, "Where there is no truth, when you take a lie to the market it will sell." Nigeria's potential to take the lead in truth-telling has been undermined. This attitude is reflected in the account of a Fulani man on the radio programme 'Tell the Truth'. Asked about why the conflict between Nigerian farmers and herders is on the increase, he said that an underlying reason is the lack of truth-telling. His kinsmen are not ready to own the truth and neither are the farmers. The lies that are told make it extremely difficult to stop the raiding and killing that is happening across the country.

In a multi-layered society like Nigeria, those who follow Christ must show that they are called to be 'salt' and 'light' and so to influence this society which has lost its way.

Our God is a God of grace, kindness, love, compassion and goodness. He created us in his own image and the Bible teaches us that we are to be his image bearers, displaying his characteristics in all our dealings with our fellow human beings (see Col 3:12). Our relational God created a relational world, a world conducive to relationships. This means that we are capable of giving and receiving love, of deserving and telling the truth, of receiving and dispensing justice, as well as being able to relate and be related to. But to unlock these virtues, we have to surrender our freedom and submit to God's moral will for our lives. Then only will society become aware of God's moral and ethical values.

Meanwhile, darkness and emptiness rule the world. This is why our world is characterized by conflict. This is why there is domestic and gender-based violence and ethnic, political, economic and religious clashes. People have forgotten the source of all relationships. They have forgotten God and in so doing have lost the ability to forge relationships built on love, truth, justice and unity.

10

The Biblical Basis for Moral Values

After the painful conclusion of the last chapter, it is wonderful to note that recent studies on moral values have revealed that there is a renewed interest about the role played by the Scriptures in the Christian's moral life.[1] Anne W. Stewart asserts that since the beginning of the 20th century the subject of moral values has often been dealt with as Old Testament theology is studied. [2] This means that the following questions are being raised: Does the Bible really address the moral issues of our contemporary society? Is God's Word sufficient and specific enough to provide appropriate ethical guidelines for humanity?

Let us begin our search for answers with this reminder from Josh and Sean McDowell:

> the Bible is not just a helpful collection of nice thoughts or just another version of the truth. The Bible is God's instruction manual for living and the primary means by which God can be known.[3]

No-one and no church should therefore seek to undermine the authority of God's word with regard to issues in modern life. Terence Kennedy points out that when people put aside the word of God, their moral perception of God and his goodness to humankind becomes dulled. [4]

---

1. John Brunt and Gerald Winslow, "The Bible's Role in Christian Ethics" in Andrews University Seminary Studies, Vol. 20. No. 1 (Spring, 1982), 3.

2. Anne W. Stewart, "Moral Agency in the Hebrew Bible" in *Oxford Research Encyclopedia*. Retrieved from religion.oxfordre.com.

3. Josh and Sean McDowell, *The Unshakable Truth*. Oregon: Harvest House Publishers, 2010, 89.

4. Terence Kennedy, "The Bible and Morality" in Biblical Roots of Christian Conduct, May (2008), 35. Retrieved from compassreview.org/winter09/6.pdf.

In the light of these statements, it is clearly essential that God's people accept the authority of God's word as the primary influence in any choices they have to make. In this way God's word will be able to influence the society that they live in. This accords with the instructions we find in both the Old and New Testaments which emphasize that God's covenant people are to exert a positive moral influence on the cultures in which they live. In other words, those who call on the name of God ought to be the conscience of the rest of the world, living exemplary lives and charting the way towards moral conduct for others.[5]

But it is clear that God's map or charter is not meant only for those who acknowledge him. Nature points all humankind to their creator. We refer to this as God's 'General Revelation.' The psalmist alludes to this revelation of God when he says that creation declares the glory of God and that "the skies proclaim the work of his hands" (Ps 19:1–3). J. A. Jacob mentions that the human soul is filled with awe by the starry heavens. The arrangement of the heavenly bodies suggests there is also a moral order in creation and this leads humankind to consider that there must be a moral law which governs humankind – an order which cannot be violated with impunity.[6] This echoes what Paul wrote to the church in Rome.

> For since the creation of the world God's invisible qualities – his eternal power and divine nature – have been clearly seen, being understood through what has been made, so that people are without excuse" (Rom 1:20).

Humankind cannot therefore claim that they lack knowledge of what is right or wrong. However, it is not enough just to acknowledge this. When God is perceived as a morally perfect being, this knowledge demands both adoration and worship. However, in most societies people do not choose to do so. Instead they shun what is right.

This is why there is the need for the second type of revelation in which God reveals himself more fully. This we call his 'Special Revelation' and it supplements the general revelation and takes us a step further in our understanding. In a study on the foundations of Christian Ethics, Kunhiyop suggests that while,

---

5. Terence Kennedy, "The Bible and Morality" in Biblical Roots of Christian Conduct, May (2008), 35. Retrieved from compassreview.org/winter09/6.pdf.

6. J. A. Jacob, "The Moral Law and the Starry Heavens" in The Biblical Illustrator: Old Testament Volumes, ed. Joseph S. Exell. (London: Ages Software), 2006.

natural revelation informs the human conscience so that people can make ethical decisions and judge between right and wrong, God's revelation in scripture does not only tell us about who He is but also about how we should live.[7]

The deep purpose of both the general and the special revelation is that people should come to know God and so fulfil God's pleasure and his specific purposes in their lives. David Gooding and John Lennox point out that people need to know the purpose of humanity's existence in order to judge whether they are living as they should.

Obedience to God's word is the only way to reshape humankind's values. It alone can enable people to serve humanity better and to uphold the highest moral order. The best way therefore to know if humans are living as they should is to ask, "How well is each person fulfilling God's will?"[8]

It is however only if one accepts that humankind is created in the image of God (Gen 1:27) and therefore has the potential to live morally that one can believe it is possible to live in such a way that one fulfils God's will. Of course, there are different ideas about what being created in God's image means. Some have suggested that the image of God is reflected in our ability to think and to make decisions. Others think that the image of God in man refers to humankind's original moral purity.[9] Whatever meaning one chooses to adopt, the fact that we are made in God's image has implications for many aspects of our existence.

Robert A. Payne takes our thinking a step further. He suggests that it is not possible to argue that all human beings have inherent dignity or unique value without appealing to some divine authority.[10] People are exceptional, not because humankind can reason nor because humans have the capacity to contribute meaningfully to make the world a better place, but because they are made in the image of God. That is what makes every human life sacred. In other words, the sacredness of life necessitates a higher morality.

This truth is conveyed throughout Scripture, in both the Old and the New Testaments. and is emphasized in the teachings of Jesus Christ (cf. Matthew 22:37–39).

7. Kunhiyop, *African Christian Ethics*, 46–7.

8. Gooding & Lennox, *The Bible and Ethics*, 4–5.

9. Wayne Grudem, Systematic Theology: An Introduction to Biblical Doctrine. Michigan: Zondervan, 2000, 443.

10. Robert Pyne, "Humanity and Sin" in *Understanding Christian Theology* eds., Charles R. Swindoll & B. Zuck (Nashville: Thomas Nelson, 2003), 683.

The Decalogue (Exod 20:3–17): Moral Values in the Old Testament

The Ten Commandments were given so that God's people would be able to make sound moral judgments about practical matters. God's laws were not vague and ethereal, but dealt with practical matters. Dwight L. Moody observes that the fifth to tenth commandments highlight the distinct duties which arise from interpersonal family relations and those with one's neighbour. They are divided into offences against life, chastity, property and character.[11] It is clear therefore that the purpose of the Decalogue was to inspire right belief and worship (orthodoxy) and that this in turn should lead to right practice and conduct (orthopraxy).

The early Christians viewed the Ten Commandments as a summary of the essentials of Christian morality. But it seems that over the centuries the focus on them waned until the Reformation. As the crucifixes and other ornaments of the pre-Reformation era were removed from the walls of the churches, their place was taken by the words of the Ten Commandments. Subsequently, Christians were required to learn the Commandments by heart in Catechism in preparation for Confirmation.[12] It also became general practice to rehearse the commandments in Sunday schools and, to ensure that they were remembered, the commandments were written on placards which were placed on the walls of church buildings.

The commands of the Decalogue still serve as a reminder of the moral discipline required of the Christian. This summary of behaviour must be preserved for the generations of all people to come. (Some Jews suggest that the reason God gave the laws in the wilderness – and not in the land which he had prepared for Israel – was because he was indicating that the law was for all nations and not exclusively for Israel.) The moral values put forward in this Old Testament perspective are not merely sacred information to be preserved, but are his divine commandments that promise rewards for obedience and consequences for disobedience. While obedience to these divine injunctions results in moral behaviour, violation of them leads to a moral decay among individuals and in the society at large. It was with this realisation that the Psalmist admitted his guilt and sinfulness (see Ps 51) and sought divine transformation.

God's covenant people can be sure that God's moral requirements are within their reach (see Deut 30:11, 14). However, the ability to be obedient

---

11. Dwight L. Moody, *Weighed and Wanting*, (Northern Ireland: Revival Publishing, 2012), 13.

12. Joyce G. Baldwin, "The Role of the Ten Commandments," Vox Evangelica 13 (1983), 7.

and to choose to behave in accordance with God's will is only possible when our hearts are right with God. When we concentrate on God's teaching about how to live wisely, when we reflect on Scripture's sacred songs and prayers, we will be able to walk to God's drum beat. And what is more, we shall be able to influence the world in which we live. Those who obey God's moral standards are not only transformed by them; they also become agents of transformation. Moral power will emanate from good deeds and upright character.

Moral Values in the New Testament

The New Testament also provides insights about moral values. In the teachings of Jesus Christ which we refer to as the Beatitudes, we are provided with new insights into the moral law of the Old Testament. For instance, Jesus says: "You have heard that it was said, 'Eye for eye, and tooth for tooth.' But I tell you, do not resist an evil person. . . . You have heard that it was said, 'Love your neighbour and hate your enemy.' But I tell you, love your enemies and pray for those who persecute you" (Matt 5:38–44). Despite these radical statements, Jesus was quick to emphasize that his messianic mission was not to abolish the Law or the teachings of the prophets but to fulfil these teachings. (Matt 5:17). John L. Mackay explains that, "Jesus did not set aside the moral law. Far from it; he warned against diluting any of the least of its commands. He considered the moral law as an abiding revelation of what right conduct and goodness involve."[13] Jesus' interpretation of the Law explains the writings of the Old Testament, adding a further dimension to our understanding of their moral value. In so doing he confirms the words of the Psalmist who says "The law of the LORD is perfect . . . trustworthy . . . right . . . radiant." (Ps 19:7–8).

In Matthew 5:13–16, Jesus reminds those who believe in him that they are to be moral influences upon the earth. He says, "You are the salt of the earth. . . . You are the light of the world." The analogy of salt and light implies that believers are called to be actively involved in society and not isolated from it. Christians must influence the world where they live. Thus we see that our spiritual life and our involvement in society cannot be separated. Edwards elaborates, suggesting that, "A Christianity which does not begin with the individual will never begin; likewise a Christianity which ends with the individual will soon die."[14] Consequently, the life of the individual Christian

---

13. John L. Mackay, *Moral Law* (Newcastle: The Christian Institute, 2017), 43.
14. Edwards, *Agenda for Change*, 10.

and the life of the church must not be isolated from non-Christian society. There must be a constant and regular attempt to engage with non-Christians.

The teachings of Jesus set the ethical and moral standards for all society. He talks about issues such as murder, lust, divorce, revenge, love for enemy and forgiveness. (Matt 5:21–48) A critical examination of these teachings reveals that he sets a higher moral standard than that which was traditionally understood and accepted. So, we learn that anger is equivalent to murder and lust to adultery, while believers are to turn the other cheek rather than take revenge. We learn that giving to the needy must be done without show and ostentation. Although these moral standards set the bar quite high, God did not command anything which was not attainable.[15]

God's high standards reveal the difference between his ways and the so-called moral practices of the people in the world. Jesus puts it like this,

> If you love those who love you, what reward will you get? Are not even the tax collectors doing that? And if you greet only your brothers, what are you doing more than others? Do not even pagans do that? Be perfect, therefore, as your heavenly Father is perfect. (Matt 5:46–48).

The apostle Paul writes extensively about moral values in his letters to the churches in the New Testament. Because the integrity of the gospel is at stake, Paul focuses both on leaders knowing the truth of the gospel and on how one should act because of this knowledge.

Notice how the behaviours he is concerned about are still reflected in today's society. The issues he was dealing with are as troublesome today as they were then. Living according to these standards would influence our role in society just as radically as it did in the world of the early Christians.

In his epistle to Timothy, for instance, Paul warns against greed and the love for money; he encourages Timothy rather to pursue righteousness, godliness, faith, love, endurance and gentleness (2 Tim 2).

Paul also deals with sexuality. Some people might prefer sex to be a private matter, but if the kingdom of God were silent about sex, people would be profoundly disappointed.[16] Paul goes so far as to command the church in Corinth that the immoral should be expelled from fellowship (1 Cor 5). The morality of the community of believers must not be corrupted by bad company.

---

15. Mark Miller, "Living Ethically in Christ:" in *Review* Vol. 27, No.1 March (1999), 21.

16. Edward T. Welch, "The Apostle Paul: On Sex" in *The Journal of Biblical Counselling*, Fall (2005), 14.

Richard L. Pratt, Jr. suggests that Paul's command could be summarized as "You are pure, so start acting like it." [17]

The New Testament also provides directions with regard to the believer's relationship with civic leadership. In the letter to the church in Rome, Paul counsels that, everyone must "be subject to the governing authorities, for there is no authority except that which God has established" (Rom 13:1). John Jefferson Davis explains that the believer's submission to the state is often misconstrued. Being subject to the authorities does not mean blind obedience to leaders that go against the commands contained in God's Word. Where the laws of men contradict the law of God, believers are admonished to choose to obey God rather than people. Leaders are God's servants and therefore must be accountable to him for their conduct.[18] Yusufu Turaki reminds us that "Good governance must comply with God's law that governs his creation and humanity. Thus every state should recognise its moral accountability to God and to its citizens."[19] When a government or constituted authority fails to conform to God's law, citizens are left with no option but civil disobedience.

We see this obedience to God in practice when Peter and his colleagues were arrested and jailed by the Sanhedrin for refusing to obey the order not to preach in the name of Jesus. They were unapologetic in their response that they must obey God rather than men (Acts 5:29). In a commentary, F. F. Bruce observes that "the authority of the Sanhedrin was great, but the authority of Him who had commissioned them to make this good news known was indeed greater."[20]

Similarly, Bernhard Christensen's study on Dietrich Bonhoeffer shows us that Bonhoeffer took up the cross of resistance against Adolf Hitler's regime even though he knew it would probably mean death. Bonhoeffer's action was in obedience to Christ.[21] Today Bonhoeffer is remembered as one who died as a martyr for Christ.

---

17. Richard L. Pratt, Jr. "A Situation of Immorality: 1 Corinthians 5:1–13" in *IIIM Magazine Online*, Volume 3, No. 38, September 17 to September 23 (2001), 63 Retrieved from thirdmill.org/articles/ric.

18. John Jefferson Davis, *Evangelical Ethics: Issues Facing The Church Today* (New Jersey: Presbyterian and Reformed Publishing Company, 2004), 223.

19. Yusufu Turaki, "The Church and the State" in *Africa Bible Commentary*, ed. Tokunboh Adeyemo (Nairobi: World Alive Publishers, 2006), 1371.

20. F.F. Bruce, *The Book of the Acts* (Grand Rapids: Eerdmans, 1954), 121.

21. Bernhard Christensen, *The Inward Pilgrimage: An Introduction to Christian Spiritual Classics*, (Minneapolis: Augsburg Publishing House, 1996), 143.

But New Testament teaching does not demand that Christians are not to participate in civic affairs. We are meant to share the light of Christ with the world, including the fields of civic affairs and politics. Writing many years ago, St Augustine concluded that, although Christians are not of this world, nevertheless while they are still in the world, it is vital that they find a balance between heavenly-mindedness and global relevance.[22] This is echoed by Paul Helm who argues that Christians should make the most of their rights and privileges in society. [23]

Clearly, we as believers cannot doubt the fact that God's word speaks with authority about moral values. Biblical standards must be upheld unapologetically by the community of God's people, the church. No Christian should be deterred from following God's ways because of the pluralistic views of our contemporary society. Relativism, which refutes absolute standards on the grounds that one's behaviour is based on where and when and who one is, must be challenged. The eternal word of God makes it clear that there are absolute standards of truth and morality. And the word of God surpasses the wisdom and philosophy of even the most enlightened ages. Loren Cunningham and Janice Rogers point out that, throughout history, the record is clear: when people have God's Word and apply what it teaches in their lives, the nation is transformed.[24] There is therefore no better standard for moral values than the Holy Bible.

It would be naïve to think that one publication could change society! However, we can take comfort from the fact that God does not necessarily work through dramatic gestures, even though he could do so. Instead he chooses to use us to fulfil his purposes. This book is part of my contribution, but each of us is charged with the task of working to create the Nigeria God intended, even though our contribution may be small and insignificant.

---

22. Saint Augustine, *The City of God* trans., Marcus Dod (New York: The Modern Library, 1950), 695.

23. Paul Helm, "Christianity and Politics in a Pluralistic Society: An Augustinian Approach" in Tales of Two Cities: *Christianity and Politics* ed. Stephen Clark., (Leicester: Inter-Varsity Press, 2005), 208.

24. Loren Cunningham and Janice Roggers, *The Book That Transform Nations: The Power of The Bible to Change any Country* (Seattle: YWAM Publishing, 2007), 22.

Section Four

Achieving Morality

We have considered the current situation in Nigeria. We have looked at the problems. We have outlined some of the attempts that have been made to remedy the situation. Now with this wealth of background, we must consider specifics about how we must live if we wish to stop the decline in morality in our society. For, of course moral values are not lived out in a vacuum; they operate in society where one's behaviour is judged as either right or wrong, good or evil.

People disagree about how society formulates which values it will adopt. Some people suggest that these moral values are derived from the society itself in order to perpetuate the norms of that society and to maintain its peace and order. This means that each society will follow its own laws and its own codes of behaviour. Others suggest that it is not society but individuals who decide on moral values. In his article, "morality" David J. Atkinson outlines this view:

> The moral behaviour of people may be shaped by their own moral character which itself is affected by their genetic make-up, by their early learning experiences, by the life choices they make and by the ideals towards which they strive. It may be shaped also by the social context in which their behaviour is set and by the nature of their relationship with significant other people in their lives.[1]

---

1. *New Dictionary of Christian Ethics and Pastoral Theology, s.v.*

Nwauzor Adaku argues that

> Moral values influence the behaviour of people within a particular
> social environment. [They] serve as a yardstick for assessing
> human behaviour. [They] entail qualitative standards of behaviour
> which affect people's actions and inactions. [They] also determine
> the harmony and disharmony in society . . . whenever something
> seriously goes wrong in the society, politicians, teachers, parents
> and religious leaders are reminded of their duty to support the
> authority of moral values in the society."[2]

Kwabena Amponsah argues that

> As people grow, they undergo several forms of experiences and
> through the acquired experiences they learn to fashion a moral
> code of behavior. What is right or wrong therefore is simply the
> result of these experiences." [3]

If this is an accurate reflection of how we come by our values, it shows why
society struggles to formulate a uniform concept of right and wrong. There
will then be as many different ideas about what is right as there are people!

Whatever view we adopt, however, it is clear that moral values are an
inherent aspect of human nature. This leads Dieter Bimbacher[4] to postulate
that it is not accurate to say that the values in society have been weakened.
He argues that even those who do wrong or who promote wrongdoing have
values. They value things such as money, reputation or even just good food.
The problem we face in engaging with society is not that the people around
us do not value anything, but that they value the wrong things. Their values
cause them to set the wrong priorities and it is probable that some of their
values are of no benefit to society as a whole.

Scott B. Rae sums this up when he says:

> Some of our values are formed either in reaction to or affirmation
> of the social conditions of the time. Unfortunately, these values can
> be mistaken for absolute standards when in reality they are a little
> more of cultural myths and biases dressed up in moral language.[5]

---

2. Adaku, "Changing Values in Contemporary Nigeria" 104–111.

3. Amponsah, *Topics on West African*, 84.

4. Dieter Birnbacher, "Moral and Other Values"

5. Rae, *Moral Choices*, 93.

Yet, because moral values underpin every aspect of human behaviour, the present and future development of any society depends on the moral values which the people there uphold.

One of the problems which hinder us as we seek to build a moral society is the fact that beliefs and assumptions tend to remain unchanged despite changes in lifestyles or even religious conversions. This is why today some Africans still hold tenaciously to certain traditional beliefs and assumptions and use these to determine the morality of their actions. These oral traditions or traditional beliefs lead to actions and rituals which define their identity as a people.

Clearly our values are firmly interwoven into our lives. This is why they can be used as a yardstick to measure our society's progress or retrogression. M. U. Ushe laments that,

> In the Nigerian context as well as Africa, people easily misunder-stand and grossly undermine the relationship between moral values and development.[6]

Cultures that misconstrue or undermine the relationship between their moral values and their development must face the consequences and will pay a heavy price for their lack of awareness. After all, common sense should teach thinking people to welcome values such as love, truth-telling, humility, honesty, integrity and industriousness. Not only are such values good in themselves, but they will also enable our societies to prosper. Thus someone who refuses to work may not see his or her action as having consequences or even as violating any moral law. Similarly, people may not see that actions such as their inappropriate disposal of waste materials (littering), involvement in sex for money, institutionalised gambling, or even amassing dubious wealth in a public office or through a ghost-workers scam affect society. Nonetheless, such acts of behaviour are indicators of moral and spiritual corruption and will hamper the development of society unless we act or speak out.

Transparency International, although it is a secular agency, knows that there are consequences when a society does not take moral values seriously. A recent Corruption Perception Index (CPI) reveals a gloomy picture for Africa and for Nigeria in particular. In 2017, Nigeria ranked 148 out of 180 countries assessed on the annual Corruption Perception Index.[7] That is a staggering statistic, one which raises concern about the development of the continent.

---

6. Ushe, "Role of Traditional African," 2.

7. Oladeinde Olawoyin, "Perception of Corruption Worsens in Nigeria: Transparency International Report" Premium Times February 22, 2018, Retrieved from *https://www.premiumtimesng.com* (Accessed February 11, 2019).

However, we know that their findings reflect the truth. Some of the corruption in Nigeria can be traced back to the character flaws of leaders who allow or allowed dishonest policies to flourish. While seeking votes from the masses, greedy politicians make laudable promises but fail to fulfil their promises. What is more, the misappropriation of public funds has become the order of the day in Nigeria. Government officials are adept at inflating the price of projects exorbitantly so many can receive kick-backs. We can all recall hearing news stories about such things. Reports about scams come through all the time. In 2015, for instance, Ameh Comrade Godwin reported that the Lagos State government claimed to have spent ₦139 million in the drilling of two boreholes at Lagos House, Ikeja.[8] More recently, Juliet Ebirim and Adetutu Adesoji reported a scam in which a snake was alleged to have swallowed ₦36 million from the JAMB office. This incident occurred despite the fact that the ruling administration's mantra was fighting corruption.[9]

It is unfortunate that headlines like these are soon suppressed and that the people involved in scandals like these ensure that such issues remain buried. When other issues of concern arise, people forget about previous crimes or atrocities. In fact, some citizens accept it as standard practice that those in authority will abuse society. There is also a tendency for individuals to see their acts of immorality as a normal way of life. They do not see themselves as answerable or accountable to any higher authority. Even patriotic people then begin to wonder whether values such as honesty and financial integrity are still important. When a culture does not have guiding principles which force its members to ensure that their actions make a contribution to the common good of the society, private morality may govern all that is done.

As Christians, however, we believe that moral duty is neither self-imposed nor imposed by social expectations; rather it is God-given.[10] When individuals scorn and make light of divine laws and principles, society is at risk. When a society sets aside godly values and instead embraces what is convenient to its own human selfish desires, such a society is on a journey to destruction.

---

8. Godwin, "Fashola Spent ₦139 Million on two Boreholes: Lagos State Government" *Daily Post* August 24, 2015. Retrieved from *dailypost.ng*.

9. Juliet Ebirim and Adetutu Adesoji, "Snake Allegedly Swallows ₦36 Million from JAMB Office Vault, Nigerians React" Vanguard February 17, 2018. Retrieved from *https://www.vanguardngr.com*

10. Holmes, *Ethics: Approaching Moral Decisions*, 102.

11

The Impact of the Loss of Morality on National Development

There are always serious consequences when moral values are disregarded. Forward-thinking individuals and nations that make transforming their society an urgent item on their agenda admit that moral integrity and development go together. This makes it clear that the call for moral integrity is not to be limited to a select few.

This becomes apparent when we consider the secrets behind the successes achieved by the western nations. The key to Western Europe's transformation was education, and a major focus of that education was character formation. This was sparked by the Judeo-Christian belief that:

> God is holy; he has given us moral laws, such as the Ten Commandments. That obedience to God's Word is the precondition of peace and the source of good life; disobedience to God's moral law is sin that does not go unpunished, but that sinners can repent and receive forgiveness and new life.
>
> . . .
>
> This good news became the intellectual foundation of the modern West, the force that produced moral integrity, economic prosperity, and political freedom.[1]

Values were not just regarded as discussion points. The leaders of these nations recognized that values had the potential to transform society. Consider,

---

1. Mangalwadi, *Truth and Transformation*, 28–29.

for example, the state of England in the early eighteenth century; it was as corrupt as many countries in modern-day Africa. However, the religious revival led by John Wesley was a major factor in England's transformation. The gospel which Wesley preached was rooted in the moral absolutes of God's law: that God takes sin seriously; that Christ became man so that he could take away our sin and its consequences; and that Jesus Christ died on the cross of Calvary so that we might find forgiveness and eternal life. When these truths were acknowledged by the masses, a culture of trustworthiness grew and with that came economic progress.

A similar pattern was seen in the Netherlands. After the reformation the Heidelberg Catechism became a primary source of doctrine in the churches here. This catechism had been drafted both to guide pastors and to instruct the youth, and it rapidly became the most influential and most generally used document of the Reformation.[2] It is worth our while to take a moment to examine just how it proclaimed the moral precepts of Scripture. Take for instance the discussion on the commandment "You shall not steal."

Question: What does God forbid in the eighth commandment?

Answer: God forbids not only outright theft and robbery punishable by law. But in God's sight theft also includes all deceitful tricks and devices, whereby we design to appropriate to ourselves anything belonging to our neighbour – whether it be by force or means that appear legitimate such as inaccurate measurements of weight, size, or volume; fraudulent merchandising; counterfeit money; excessive interest; or any other means forbidden by God. In addition, God forbids all greed and pointless squandering of his gifts.

Question: But what does God require in this commandment?

Answer: That I do whatever I can for my neighbour's good, that I treat others as I would like them to treat me, and that I work faithfully so that I may share with those in need.[3]

The Heidelberg Catechism was not adding anything to the commandments in Scripture. God himself had told his people that those who did not tithe were robbing him (Mal.3:8). As a result of taking God's comment seriously, generation after generation in the Netherlands were taught to work hard and to give tithes and offerings to God (Eph 4:28).[4] As a result, the country is among the top ten donor countries when it comes to foreign aid. The 2017 statistics of the Development Assistance Committee, (which was created to

---

2. *The Heidelberg Catechism,* Page 519.

3. *The Heidelberg Catechism,* 552

4. Mangalwadi, *Truth and Transformation,* 34.

oversee and discuss issues regarding foreign aid) reveal that the Netherlands donated $4.96 billion to Ethiopia, South Sudan, Afghanistan, Bangladesh, Rwanda, Yemen, Mali, Mozambique, Syria and Benin.[5] The importance that the country attached to hard work, honesty and their genuine concern for their 'neighbours' meant both that they were able to give to other countries and that they themselves became prosperous. Even today, although the church is weak in the Netherlands, the citizens demonstrate a commitment to these same Christian values and the country reaps the benefits.

It is sad therefore to hear Maier's lament that,

> with the increasing secularization of society and the current emphasis on multiculturalism especially in religious matters; the massive impact that Christianity has had on civilization is often overlooked, obscured, or even denied.

Moral values enable a nation to prosper. When citizens are intentionally taught to cultivate the right habits, their nations are exalted. In contrast, when the moral values of a nation are on the decline, the nation will experience political instability. Society will be rocked by the dysfunctionality of its families and even by the killing of innocent people.

Our lack of awareness of the radical power of the Christian gospel means that we are allowing ourselves to drift away from its values. As a result, the fabric of our society and indeed of our nations is being destroyed. If we want to stop this freefall, we must scrutinize our values and discard those that are not helping us advance as a society and a nation.

This will impact on our choice of leaders as Mark Rutland explains:

> The most basic values held by a society dictate the kind of leaders it will produce. If the premier values are hard work, perseverance, ingenuity and discipline, that society will produce good leaders.[6]

The implication is that, if we are prepared to tolerate laziness, dishonesty and a lack of discipline, our leaders will be incompetent and our society will become unproductive.

In a study on the need to reconsider the values we set ourselves, Donatus Njoku stresses the consequences of diminishing moral values. He suggests that the loss of morality can lead citizens to pursue wealth without knowledge or

---

5. Michele Wheat, "Which Countries Provide and Receive the Most Foreign Aid?" in WristBand Resources retrieved from wristband.com/content/which-countries-provide-receive-most-foreign-aid/

6. Rutland, *Character Matters*, 6.

character, pleasure without conscience, commerce without morality, worship without sacrifice, science without humanity and politics without principles.[7] Donatus I. Njoku further argued that when the value system of a nation crumbles, the disciplines and practices that should lead to development and stability also disappear. He writes,

> The crisis of the value system in Nigeria suggests that the growth and progress of the society is being retarded in many aspects through materialistic tendencies. Materialism has taken over government and political institutions in the country. It has also invaded traditional and cultural institutions, while the religious places seem to be more materialistic than the secular society. The malady of value crisis has predicated Nigeria as an open society in which anything goes. There is a high level of distrust and suspicion to the extent that everybody has become a suspect of misplaced value. Immorality and lack of sanctity of life have continued to increase as suicide, banditry, murder and kidnapping have become a daily occurrence that pervades the society. One thing remains sacrosanct, the dominant traits in the character of Nigerians should remain the overriding values of the people and the nation. Nigerians must therefore return to the era where they extolled good values; they must become a people with genuine love for one another and stop the killing of fellow Nigerians at the slightest provocation. Nigeria should become a nation where Nigerians can accommodate and accept one another's belief, culture and general way of life.[8]

Blessing Nonye Onyima asserts that,

> the value system has gradually been eroded as issues like respect for elders, chastity, integrity and morality are considered archaic, while wrong values like disrespect, disobedience, nudity, fraud, kidnapping, corruption are entrenched in the society.[9]

It is encouraging to note however that there are still those who believe that the Nigeria our founding fathers envisioned can still be actualized. Unfortunately, it is difficult to pinpoint any practical ways in which national

---

7. Njoku, "Re-Orientation of Value System, 25.

8. Njoku, "Re-Orientation of Value System," 25–32.

9. Blessing Nonye Onyima, "Nigerian Cultural Heritage: Preservation, Challenges and Prospects" *New Journal of African Studies*. https://www.ajol.info/index.php/og/article/viewFile/141270/131004

values are being instilled into the hearts of Nigerians! Instead the things that are promoted most often are narratives that trigger hatred and disunity. In an article on investments that could make Nigeria great again, Dike Chukwumerije laments that,

> We've been told that the Igbos killed the Sardauna. You were not told that the Sardauna was killed by Major Kaduna Nzeogu [who was not an Igbo man]. You're told that the Yorubas betrayed the Igbos. You're not told that Obafemi Awolowo [a Yoruba] was the Commissioner of Finance in Gowon's government during the war and it was his responsibility to involve a physical strategy for the Nigerian side in the civil war. And so we keep seeing our social reality through the blinkers of this story, which forces us to keep interpreting current facts using models that were invented fifty years ago.[10]

It is high time we invested in values that can unite us and enable us to move forward. It is high time we stopped politicizing our ethnic and religious differences. Instead our focus should be on the things we have in common. True, there are the challenges we share: we have bad roads in common; there are no books in our public schools; there are no drugs in our hospitals; poverty and corruption are widespread. However, we also have values in common. These are the values contained in our National Anthem.

Consider, for instance, the call to compatriots to serve the fatherland with 'love and strength and faith'. This does not mean that the citizens must begin something new; instead the call asks them to continue the work of those who laboured in the past. If we do this, the nation will be bound together in freedom, peace and unity. The Pledge puts it differently, but the emphasis is the same. It charges Nigerians to be 'faithful, loyal and honest; to serve the nation with all of one's strength and to defend the nation's unity and uphold the nation's honour and glory with God's help.'

Our collective responsibility to achieve the Nigeria of our dreams should be to invest in these moral values. In other words, although we benefit from our partnership with the global village, we must also revisit and protect our traditional values that are of national benefit.

When our nation was formed, the principles and values that we aspired to gave us hope. It is high time we revisited those values and vowed to uphold them once again as dearly as if they were a form of catechism or a statement of belief.

---

10. Dike Chukwumerije, "Six Investments that Could."

12

Promote Non-Violence

One of the moral values we must consider is our attitude to violence. Nonviolence is not popular today but Christians are required to play their part in breaking the cycle of violence in our country. Many people perceive nonviolence as mere passivity. Many Christians therefore think that Jesus is asking us to fold our hands and do nothing even when our murderous enemies physically attack us. They do not realize that nonviolence involves a lot of hard work. They do not realize that responding to violence requires us to use our intelligence. Through prayer and spiritual diligence we are to search out different ways of responding, to search for better options, to submit to God's guidance so that his divine power will work through us. Paul, speaking to Christians living in a violent world, puts it like this:

> Though we live in the world, we do not wage war as the world does. The weapons we fight with are not the weapons of the world. On the contrary, they have divine power to demolish strongholds. We demolish arguments and every pretension that sets itself up against the knowledge of God and we take captive every thought to make it obedient to Christ (2 Corinthians 10:3–5).

That makes it clear that nonviolence is not passivity. Instead it involves proactive engagement in dialogue and discourses that will ultimately enable us to bring about change through the building and maintenance of trust, justice and peace.

We know both from the Bible and history that in Jesus's day, conflict and victimisation were everyday occurrences in Israel. Jesus was ministering to people who were humiliated and denied their rights. By and large, their human dignity was disregarded. The Jewish people hated their Roman conquerors and longed to revenge the insults of their rule. Even his closest disciples could not get their heads around the fact that Jesus did not resist his capture and crucifixion. But his example backed up the radical ideas he had taught his followers.

Jesus had been utterly consistent in his attitude. He had taught that his followers were not to "resist an evil person," but must "turn . . . the other cheek" (Matt 5:39). They must go "the extra mile" (Matt 5:41). They were to "love" their enemies. They must "forgive" those who persecuted them and, instead of taking vengeance, they must pray for them (Matt 5:43). They were to "be as shrewd as snakes and as innocent as doves" (Matt 10:16). Thus they were, in the words of Paul, not to be "overcome by evil, but [to] overcome evil with good" (Rom 12:21).

When Jesus told them to seek first the Kingdom of God and his righteousness (Matt 6:33), he was reminding them that his followers were to have a different attitude from those around them. They belonged to a different kingdom, a kingdom of righteousness, godliness, faith, love, endurance and gentleness. His words have stood as a signpost throughout the ages for those who love and follow him. Although obeying them is easier said than done, the reign of God in our lives makes it possible.[1] This was revolutionary teaching then. These teachings are still revolutionary. But we cannot disregard them if we call ourselves his followers and they are very relevant to us in Nigeria today.

Jesus's disciples followed what they had been taught. They remained resolute in the face of persecution. Led by Peter, the early apostles stood firm in the Lord, choosing to endure persecution non-violently because they understood that this was what following Jesus meant and they loved their Lord deeply.

The picture becomes even clearer when we refer to the early chapters of Genesis. When God created Adam and Eve, he created communities: first, between himself and humankind, second, between men and women, and third, between humankind and the environment. God established order and obedience to sustain these relationships. However, when the law was broken, these relationships were shattered.

Thus, the Fall brought violence, conflict and hostility into the world. At the heart of every dispute, every war, every violent conflict and every bitter accusation is a broken relationship. Broken homes, dysfunctional families, excessive use of corporal punishment or force, incest, rape are all confirmations of the reality of evil in our world. Few, if any, relationships are free from selfish motives. Revenge and hatred are always easier than peace and love.

---

1. Glen H. Stassen and David Gushee, *Kingdom Ethics: Following Jesus in Contemporary Context* (Grand Rapids: Eerdmans, 2002, 2016), 21.

Even in the church, the vigilante spirit is alive and well. Some Christians sometimes attempt to sanctify their anger by calling it righteous indignation, because as humans we too are tempted to retaliate against those who mistreat us. Piously, some believers may even invoke Romans 12:9 as a proof text for our revenge—as long as we read no further in Romans.[2]

To counteract our knee-jerk reaction to respond to violence with violence, it is important that we know how we got to where we are today in Nigeria. Many Nigerian Christians believe that the primary reason they are persecuted is that the Muslims want to implement their agenda of Islamising the entire country. This, however, is not the whole truth. Satan's tactic of twisting the truth is still at work in Nigeria, just as it was in Eden. Social media, the internet, the movies, for instance, have all become avenues for sharing and propagating fake news across the globe. Photo-shopped pictures of atrocities in other parts of the world suggest that attacks are local. We are denied the real picture and end up consuming half-truths.

The underlying truth is that, as the African concept of evil demonstrates and as the Bible confirms, evil manifests itself in broken relationships. Years of wars and violent conflicts, together with traumas which have never been dealt with, are hurting our present-day relationships. We are suffering the consequences of our unforgiving and unrepentant hearts. We could even say we are bewitched by our emotions. This lack of forgiveness means we are vulnerable when we hear fake news. So when we are told that the Muslims are hiring mercenaries to attack all Christian communities across Nigeria so that they can successfully claim the country for Islam, we believe these reports utterly. There may be some element of truth in those messages, but much of their content is false. Those who spread these reports are damaging us. They are, in reality, launching a frontal attack on the values that Jesus taught. And Jesus's values of love, truth, justice and unity are the very ideas which feature in our national anthem and our pledge! They are the virtues that secure creational relationships.

Although, as in the beginning, transgressions must be punished, reconciliation and restoration should be pursued. This is what God expects of us. This is what Christ did for us when he died on the cross to restore us to a right relationship with our Creator God.

---

2. Loving Your Enemies: Overcoming Evil with Good. https://bible.org/seriespage/32-loving-your-enemies-overcoming-evil-good-romans-1214-21.

The Challenges to Living Nonviolently

In a world full of violence, it is hard to think of any option other than to respond to violence with violence. In many respects, violence seems to be the logical way to go.

The many dangers in life which threaten to kill us compound this feeling. We are fearful of undisciplined drivers on our terrible roads, of the unsanitary conditions and the diseases which they bring, of poisonous snakes, of thieves, of natural disasters. We dread poverty and starvation. How can we survive without protection? These types of dangers are beyond our control. Protecting ourselves is possibly simply a matter of being careful.

While the above dangers do not require us to deal with other people, there are other dangers that result from the fact that we are being attacked by our fellow humans. And it is in these circumstances that the call to respond non-violently becomes a factor; as Christians we must respond to the attacks orchestrated by Satan and his demons non-violently.

Yet, our faith is still challenged by our craving to feel protected. The provision of protection was an essential element in our traditional religions, where we would consult the ancestors and the spirits in order to be safe. And it is hard to lay aside that practice. Many Christians are still consumed by a desire or need to do something to feel safe. However, when we plan to act on our own behalf, we are refusing to face the reality of our limitations or the vulnerability which we have inherited as members of a fallen, broken and decaying world. We forget that we are not God and that as mere creatures we do not even know exactly who our most dangerous enemies are! We dare not trust our own instincts or abilities.

Fortunately, God understands this human frailty. Perhaps that is why the Bible is replete with passages that teach that the Lord is our protector. These verses show us that we need to reorient our thinking. Our natural weapons can never save us. Instead we have to learn to rely on God and to trust him to do his work in his time and in his way. This is the attitude of the psalmist when he proclaims: "Though an army besieges me, my heart will not fear; though war break out against me, even then I will be confident" (Ps 27:3). The willingness to remain resolute and to respond non-violently to the troubles that surround us is only possible when we accept that God is indeed our protector.

Sometimes, however, we are challenged by the fact that other Christians do not seem to take Christ's gospel of nonviolence seriously. Often they quote examples from Israel's wars of conquest, the stories of which fill the pages of the Old Testament, and they suggest that these accounts prove that it is acceptable to employ violence in self-defence, even if we should not go on the offensive. It is not within the scope of this chapter to point out the flaws in such arguments. There are many reference works where these matters are dealt with comprehensively.[3] Suffice to say that the Old Testament accounts do not in any way contradict the idea of non-violence. The need to rely on God's power and wisdom was a central motif even in those Old Testament wars of conquest. Time without number Israel was forced to realize that God was in charge and that he was the one who would fight their battles. David and others may have had physical weapons to use, but it was not the use of these weapons which brought them success. Instead, when they looked to God for victory, God intervened miraculously. We could cite numerous examples in which the weapons of Israel remained sheathed, but the enemy was defeated.

Our attitude to nonviolence may also be challenged by false teachers who preach another Jesus, a different gospel. There are those in our Christian ranks who believe and act as though they are "Super Apostles" or "Super Christians." To these 'Super Christians' nonviolence is not an option. They are proud rather than humble, and they crave the popularity that action will bring them. When pride takes over like this, their foolishness leads them to believe that they have been assigned the task of protecting their flock. In fact, they begin to doubt whether God is really capable of protecting his own without their help! They see things from a human perspective and, as a result, they convince their followers that Christ's teaching of nonviolence cannot possibly apply in our context of enemies such as the Fulani killer-herdsmen, Boko Haram, or even our corrupt Nigerian leaders.

In fact such teachings reveal that these leaders are false apostles of Christ. They are abusing God's power. They are simply perpetuating violence. After all, one of the reasons that violent conflicts persist in Nigeria and elsewhere is that those behind them want power and authority over others. False teachers are being manipulated by evil.

Because we are so competitive by nature, we want to measure ourselves against others and compare ourselves with them. We want to gain an advantage over them. Clearly Christ's gospel of nonviolence does not fit with such a mindset. Rather it challenges Christians to put God first. Our lives need to be characterized by a careful attention to Bible reading and study, prayer, self-reflection, worship of God and service to our fellow men and women. These may include our known and unknown enemies. The Bible is our moral vision and map. As Obasanjo says, "The Bible speaks to us about God, about

---

3. See Agang, Impact of Ethnic.

the world we live in, about life and death and about ourselves."[4] It is where the moral power we need lies.

We must become like Jesus Christ. He not only embodied nonviolence through his teaching, he even went submissively to the cross to expose how much God hates violence. Paul (together with all God's children throughout the ages) is reminded that, "My power is made perfect in weakness" (2 Cor 12:9–10). Morris points out that the founder of the Methodist church, John Wesley, discovered several centuries ago that there was an amazing power which came upon God's people when small groups met together regularly to pray, to study Scriptures and to witness. He explains that Christians who take nonviolence seriously also need to unite "in order to pray together, to receive the word of exhortation, and to watch over one another in love, that they might help each other to work out their salvation."

Submission to spiritual discipline helps to prepare people to experience God's presence. Only then will they be able to put God first in every circumstance. Only then will they be able to curb their instinctive responses to provocation from those who are troublemakers in our society.

The Consequences of Violence

If we as Christians respond to evil violently, we will lose the spiritual connectedness which we need to withstand Satan's strategies in his war against God and his people. The Bible's call to respond to evil without violence is a clarion call because that is the only way to escape the temptation to worship Satan, the god of this world. Nonviolence is about preserving the truth of the gospel of Christ in our fallen, decaying and dying world.

Responding to violence with violence would mean that we had failed to realise that all evil is intrinsically connected to Satan and his demons. While evil has a physical dimension, it is essentially a spiritual power. Wink explains that evil happens at two levels:

> Every Power tends to have a visible pole, an outer form – be it a church [mosque, temple, shrine, etc], a nation, or an economy – and an invisible pole, an inner spirit or driving force that animates, legitimates, and regulates its physical manifestation in the world.[5]

Later in his book, Wink illustrates this concept by referring to a football match:

---

4. Obasanjo, *This Animal Called Man*, xi.
5. Wink, *Naming the Powers*, 5.

A "mob spirit" does not hover in the sky waiting to leap down on unruly crowds at a soccer match. It is the actual spirit constellated when the crowd reaches a certain critical flashpoint of excitement and frustration. It comes into existence at that moment, causes people to act in ways of which they would never have dreamed of themselves capable, and then ceases to exist the moment the crowd disperses .. ... An ideology does not just float in the air; it is always the nexus of legitimations and rationales for some actual entity, be it union or management, a social change group or the structure it hopes to change. As the inner aspect of material reality, the spiritual powers are everywhere around us. Their presence is real, and it is inescapable. The issue is not whether we "believe" in them but whether we can learn to identify our actual, everyday encounters with them – what Paul called 'discerning the spirits.'"[6]

If we respond to evil in a way which will displease our Lord, we are being influenced not by 'good' but by evil. A violent response to anyone means we are deviating from the moral vision of our Lord. Yet if we claim to be his followers, we must follow in his footsteps. When we gave our lives to Jesus Christ, we essentially surrendered our lives to God. We implicitly renounced a life of violence. We have died to the law of violence. We must therefore "do good to those who hate [us]" (Luke 6:27). Paul puts it like this:

I have been crucified with Christ. It is no longer I who live, but Christ who lives in me. And the life I now live in the flesh I live by faith in the Son of the God, who loved me and gave himself for me." (Gal 2:20 ESV)

When we are daunted by this task, it is important to remember that, because Christ entrusted the church with the gospel of nonviolence, we can depend on him for the power to live that way. We can live without retaliating violently if we depend on God's power and generous grace.

---

6. Wink, *Naming the Powers*, 103. 105–106.

13

What Else Can We Do?

Promote a Work Ethic

Previously we mentioned the work ethic in the Netherlands, noting that one of the hallmarks of a successful nation is that its citizens are taught to see their work as something that must be cherished. But Nigeria also valued work at one time.

There are two important statues in Gboko, one is at the Bristow Roundabout and the other is at the Yandev Roundabout. The one is a sculpture of a man carrying a hoe on his shoulder and a cutlass in his hand; the other depicts a man lifting up his hoe as though he wanted to plough the ground. These statues represented the work ethic of the residents of the Gboko metropolis and, because of their central position, enabled visitors to the town to see the connection between the statues and the everyday life of the residents who were mostly farmers. These pieces of art were beautifully carved and therefore revealed to both children and adults that work was honourable and admirable. They reminded people that those who labour or work with their hands are important. They aimed to encourage the people not to be idle but to work so that they would have what they needed with enough to spare for those who did not. The elders in the town valued hard work and worked diligently, and the younger generation followed their example.

Unfortunately, today the narrative has changed. Today there are some who do not believe that they have to work at all. They simply believe that they have the right to rely on others to cater for their needs or, failing that, that they have the right to support themselves by begging for alms.

Moreover the numbers of those who believe in hard work are declining constantly. This change is not peculiar to the residents of Gboko; it has rapidly become a national attitude. In a study on the work ethic of Nigerian workers, P.

S. Olowolaju asserts that, for many people, work is the least rewarding part of their lives. The time they spend at work is described as "hours of endurance" rather than "hours of pleasure." Work is a "necessary evil;" something which has to be done to earn a living but which brings little personal satisfaction.[7]

In order to find satisfaction in work, we must change our perspective. In a study on practicing the Christian faith in the workplace, Craig and Matthew T. Bishop assert that, irrespective of our position, we can work for God, work like God and expect a reward from God. If we did this we would have a new perspective that would make any job more meaningful.[8]

P. A. Marshall stresses that "Human beings are responsible for the world and are to shape human culture and history. Hence explicit attention is paid to human work. Even God is described as one who makes, forms, builds, and plants."[9] This is not just an Old Testament truth for the same attitude can be seen in the New Testament. Jesus relates his teachings to the everyday world of work, while Paul condemns idleness in his letter to the church in Thessalonica (2 Thess 3:6–15).

Any nation that seeks to progress must regard work as honourable. This can inspire people to acquire new skills so that they can maximize their God-given talents, thereby perhaps becoming self-employed and being able to employ others. We must insist on teaching the younger generation the value and benefits of work. When the value of work is cherished, it is possible that we as a nation will be able to boast about our innovations and inventions.

Encourage Respect for Persons

With globalization, modernization and technological advancements it is clear that the value of human life is being eroded on a daily basis. This is why we must revisit and strengthen our respect for persons.

Lawrence Richards adds to this definition, explaining that the Bible makes it clear that the concept of respect is a far more important one than our modern day users imagine. We tend to use the word far more casually than the Bible does.[10]

---

7. Olowolaju, "The Work Ethic of Nigerian Workers."
8. Bishop & Bishop, *Faithspace in the Workplace*, 208.
9. *New Dictionary of Christian Ethics*, s.v. "work"
10. Richards, "Respect" in *New International Encyclopedia*, 523.

Respect for persons arises out of relationships. In fact, some scholars suggest that building relationships is part of what it means to be human. It is recorded that in a recent inaugural lecture, Nihinlola suggests that

> to be human is to establish and nourish relationships that will enrich other human beings in spiritual, social, cultural, economic and political dimensions of life.[11]

Clearly there are positive implications when human actions that breed harmony are encouraged. It is important to note that we should not just respect others because of what we stand to gain; instead respect should be an acknowledgement of the honour that human beings deserve. Those who acknowledge that the humanity of others is deserving of respect indirectly earn respect for themselves as they maintain the golden rule; what goes around surely comes around.

While people from other societies may struggle to admit that people are deserving of respect simply because they are human, this is not a problem for Africans. Africans generally agree that respect is of paramount importance. However, it is important to note that this value cannot be discussed in a vacuum as different cultures and individuals show their respect differently depending on their culture, their religious beliefs or their professional work.

Africans respect the elderly in particular, even though there may be no obvious reason to respect an old person. It is thought that the elderly by virtue of their age have earned the right to courtesy and politeness. This is why it is expected that early in life children will be taught to respect the elderly. Such home-based training is meant to affect their attitudes towards society as a whole, training them to be polite and courteous when dealing with others.

Ezenweke and Kanayo add to this by stating, "The elders are respected first because they are believed to be the teachers and directors of the young." The young are often told that if they respect the elders, they will be respected by the young when they become elders. Of course, this helps to uphold the customs and traditions in the society. This is why even the young Africans in the diaspora are also taught this principle. It will help them to appreciate their roots and to fit in when they visit or eventually return to Africa. This way of thinking enables one to establish and nourish interpersonal relationships between the younger and older generations.

---

11. Ezenweke & Nwadialor, "Understanding Human Relations", 62

I must point out, however, that sometimes because children are forced to be givers of respect, they are treated as if they do not have any rights or as if they are not worthy of respect. Ifeyinwa Annastasia Mbakogu states that,

> children in the African continent, have been brought up to be overtly submissive to their parents in everything that includes decisions on what should be appropriate whether right or wrong for their future growth and development.[12]

While it is good to train children to show respect, this should not imply that we should treat children as if they do not exist. (When children are left alone at home, people suggest that there is nobody there!) Unfortunately, this can lead to some children regarding themselves as nobodies and growing into adulthood without self-respect, thinking of themselves as nonentities. Children also should be treated with respect.

> One of the most common ways in which the African respect for persons can be perceived is in the manner of greetings. We believe that there is a polite and respectful way of greeting people, and it is expected that children and visitors learn and become acquainted with what is acceptable in the respective cultures. As an example, Remi Oyeyemi asserts that respect is the hallmark of the Yoruba tradition. The elderly are accorded respect without demanding for it. It is customary for the young female, for instance, to kneel down for the elders whenever they are greeting them.[13]

This culture has a religious undertone. As such the elderly enjoy respect because it is seen as a sacred duty. This means that kneeling and bowing are not merely done for show, but to show reverence. Interestingly, there are some who question the way in which the traditional Yoruba people pay "proper greetings", claiming that it suggests worshipping a fellow human being. Ajeigbe argues, however, that this is misguided.[14] Their actions merely denote respect.

---

12. Ifeyinwa Annastasia Mbakogu, "Exploring the Forms of Child Abuse in Nigeria: Efforts at Seeking Appropriate Preventive Strategies," *Journal of Social Sciences* 8/1 (2004): 27.

13. Remi Oyeyemi, "Of Respect, Integrity, and Omoluabi" culled from the internet, http://saharareporters.com/2017/11/08/respect-integrity-and-omoluabi-concept-remi-oyeyemi#:~:text=In%20Yoruba%20land%20like%20in,the%20hallmark%20of%20our%20tradition.&text=This%20principle%20is%20so%20deep,much%20protest%20from%20the%20youngster.

14. Raymond Ajeigbe, "Prostration in Yorubaland is a Greeting and not an Act of Worship" in The *Unknown Nigeria Blog*. No page. https://theunknownnigeriablog.blogspot.com

There are other cultural groups in Nigeria whose views concerning respect we should also consider. In an exposition on human dignity, Clement I. Osunwokeh opines that,

> the Igbo believe that, by according human person rights and respect, God also is recognized in his essence. Rights and respect accorded to the human person is the fulcrum of social justice."[15]

This claim might be regarded as audacious, however it carries echoes of the Judeo-Christian teaching which states that humans are created in the image of God and should be treated with respect and dignity. It is also in line with the words of Jesus Christ, "The King will reply, 'Truly I tell you, whatever you did for one of the least of these brothers and sisters of mine, you did for me'" (Matt 25:40). It is therefore right to suggest that when humankind is treated correctly, the dignity accorded to humanity forms a link with God who is the source of all human life.

An unequal society

It has been observed that Nigerian society, like most others on the African continent, is patriarchal in nature. In such a society the men are favoured and male domination is perpetuated. This marginalizes and, in some cases, completely excludes the women, keeping them in an inferior position. Safinatu Aliyu Dogo argues that in a patriarchal society the dichotomy between the masculine and feminine gender widens and that

> in all areas of society, structures are manipulated to maintain and foster this domination of women by men. In such a system, men are regarded as the authority within the areas of society like the traditional family, clan or tribe."[16]

This domination suggests that men are more deserving of respect than women. As a result, the sins of the men are often tolerated and overlooked, while those of women are not. In a sense, the patriarchal system makes the women the givers of respect, while the men are the recipients of respect. Unfortunately, the culture does not spell out why this should be so. But even though it has become the norm, any form of marginalization, suppression, oppression or segregation of women is disrespectful.

---

15. Osunwokeh, "Human Dignity Stance" 2.
16. Dogo, "Nigerian Patriarchy," 263–264.

It is important that we should insist that women and children are regarded as worthy of respect, just as the menfolk are. They too are fearfully and wonderfully made in the image of God. They too have moral worth. Therefore if we maltreat a fellow human being we are disregarding our creator. Clearly respect should be reciprocal, irrespective of who is involved; it should be shown to the young as well as to the elderly, to the women as well as to the men. Respect should not be denied to or withheld from anyone.

However, respect for persons seems to have eluded us as a nation. We greet only those we are familiar with and show respect only to those we think we can benefit from. When people hold views that are contrary to ours, we are prone to think that they do not deserve our respect. Yet we share a common humanity; we are part of the same nation. The presence of strangers in our midst should remind us that we too are 'strangers' in this world. If we were to think along these lines, we would find numerous reasons why we must extend respectful gestures to others, irrespective of their religious affiliation, ethnic background, political leanings, socioeconomic status, age or gender.

Encourage Respect for the Sanctity of Life

In light of this, it is clear that the Christian faith must also uphold the principle of respect for life. Ronald J Sider expresses this concept as follows:

> Our dignity and worth do not come from some government decision, some humanly defined quality of life, or some socially defined level of human usefulness. They come from the fact that the Creator selected human beings alone out of all the created order to bear the divine image and exercise a unique stewardship over the rest of creation.[17]

Thus, while the phrase 'the sanctity of human life' is not used in the Bible, clearly "everyone has a duty to conserve and respect human life, and to accept responsibility for the life of their fellow human."[18]

Yet today the sanctity of human life is under attack as never before. Certain modern philosophies examine the nature of humankind in a manner that erodes the sanctity of life; some of these actually raise serious questions about life. There are those who have come to the conclusion that life is just a dream;

---

17. Sider, *The Scandal of Evangelical Politics*, 146.
18. *New Dictionary of Christian Ethics & Pastoral Theology*, s.v. "Sanctity of Human Life"

others see life as useless; yet others are hedonistic, believing that life is about eating, drinking and having fun.

The way people view life determines how much respect they accord to human life. Sproul, commenting on the modern philosophy of reason, laments that science has joined with these modern philosophies and has reached some gloomy conclusions. He cites a nuclear physicist, Winston C. Duke, who asserts that,

> A philosophy of reason will define a human being as life which demonstrates self-awareness, volition and rationality. . . . Thus it should be recognized that not all men are human, it would seem to be more inhuman to kill an adult chimpanzee than a newborn baby, since the chimpanzee has greater mental awareness.[19]

This view is nothing other than an outright rejection of the truth that the Scriptures proclaim. Individuals, households and society are affected when human life is not treated with the honour and respect that God endowed it. In a recent post, Creech laments that,

> It's difficult to find any issue that has had a more harmful impact on the lives of individuals, families, and the community than the rejection of the sanctity of human life.[20]

Yet in Nigeria, the disregard for human life is increasingly disturbing. Oby Ezekwesili, who was the Presidential candidate of the Allied Congress Party of Nigeria (ACPN), expressed her dissatisfaction with the situation in Nigeria. She lamented that, among other things, under President Muhamadu Buhari the primacy of human life in Nigeria had been completely devalued. It is, she said, a country where life is cheapened.[21]

It is even more disturbing to note that those who take the law into their hands and who take the lives of their fellow Nigerians shamelessly give irrational and inhumane justifications for their actions. No matter what grievances we hold against others, we must restrain ourselves. We must not end human life. After all we cannot create life, so why should we even think of destroying it!

---

19. Winston Duke, "The New Biology", *Reason Magazine* (August 1972), 4–11, cited in Paul Fowler, *Abortion: Toward an Evangelical Consensus* (Portland: Multnomah, 1987), 36, and then cited in R.C. Sproul, *Abortion: A Rational Look at an Emotional Issue*, (Colorado: Navpress, 1990), 28.

20. Baranzke, "Sanctity of Human Life" no page.

21. Oby Ezekwesili, "The Primacy of the Human Life has Completely been Devalued under Buhari" in *Nigerian Guardian*. https://www.youtube.com/watch?v=29spOKLqWf8

Instead, we must accept as a matter of personal principle that we will give peace a chance.

This principle covers all life, including that of those who are not capable of communicating on contents and topics, and those who do not possess a self-concept or self-awareness. Some people feel that individuals in this state do not deserve to be referred to as human beings. The implications of such a point of view are enormous. It would include those whose health has failed, those who are elderly and weak, those who have special needs, as well as unborn infants. It is barbaric to judge and write such people off. Kunhiyop rejects this view outright.

> The problem with this argument is that the criterion for judging personhood is relativistic and subjective, open to different interpretations. The innocent, weak and defenseless can easily be dismissed as failing to meet the requirements for personhood. Such a view has terrible consequences: deformed babies and the elderly can be put to death without any fear of being charged with murder.[22]

Believing in the sanctity of life means that no price is too high when it comes to caring for persons with special needs or preserving a life that is dependent upon another. Christians hold this view despite the emergence of some troubling medical opinions on this matter. There are for instance, so-called progressive thinkers who argue that persons with special needs are a burden on the medical system as they drain it of the money needed for their constant care. They argue that these funds could be used for other purposes. Gibbs and Demoss summarize these opinions:

> We are told these people have no quality of life worth preserving, that any medical care would be futile for them. As the seeds of these pro-death ideas take root, the elderly as well as those suffering from dementia, epilepsy, Down syndrome, Alzheimer's, or Parkinson's disease are summarily lumped into the useless eaters pot.[23]

Baranzke gives us some idea of the extent of the problem.

---

22. Kunhiyop, *African Christian Ethics*, 337.

23. David Gibbs and Bob Demoss, *Fighting for Dear Life: The Untold Story of Terri Schiavo and What It Means for All of Us* (Minneapolis, Minnesota: Bethany House, 2006), 209.

The rejection of the sanctity of human life has led to the greatest loss of life in all of human history – from the taking of one life at a time to genocide's systematic eradication of millions. Rwanda genocide (1994): 1,174,000 Tutsi and Hutu people. Cambodia genocide (1975–1979): 2,000,000 Khmer people. The Holocaust/Shoah (1933–1945): 13,000,000 Europeans, including 6, 000,000 Jews. The Stalin regime (1941–1953): 20,000,000 Soviets and global abortion: 42,000,000 unborn children every year.[24]

It is important to emphasize that the rejection of the sanctity of human life is not merely disrespectful, but that the consequences can be disastrous. Attitudes like this have led to whole campaigns of destruction. We also see these destructive tendencies in less widespread actions, for instance in parents who pay in order to end the lives of their unborn children and in those who conceive a child merely to provide donor organs for another of their children. The list could go on and on. We could include acts like sexual abuse, sex trafficking, slavery, prostitution and rape. All of these show scant reverence for human life.

Remember to show empathy

The Focus on the Family webpage declares the following foundational principle:

> "We believe that human life is created by God in His image. It is of inestimable worth and significance in all its dimensions . . . Christians are therefore called to defend, protect, and value all human life."[25]

Jesus reminded his followers to respect others and to treat them in the best possible way, saying "Do to others as you would have them do to you" (Luke 6:31). This has become known as 'The Golden Rule.' 'Zecha attempts to clarify the meaning of these words by offering various versions, such as,

> Do to others what you yourself would like to experience, or don't do to others what you would dislike to suffer. By imaginatively putting myself into the place of the other person my own willing becomes the measure of how to treat them.[26]

24. Baranzke, "Sanctity of Human Life" no page.
25. Focus on the Family, "Sanctity of Human Life," no page.
26. Zecha, "Golden Rule in Applied," no page.

We might also call this the 'Rule of Empathy' as it requires the willingness to treat others with respect, without expecting anything in return. People ought not to be treated as a means to an end as they are indeed "fearfully and wonderfully made" (Ps 139:14a).

It is sad to observe that atrocities are increasing however. Recently major media houses and news stations announced the existence of a slave-trading syndicate in Africa through which young people were dehumanized and sold like common properties. The media described a market at which slaves could be bought for as little as 1,200 Libyan Dinar (about 250 United States Dollars)! The pictures reveal people being treated like cattle. We react with shock and repulsion. These scenes reveal a tremendous lack of empathy. It is hard to justify why people would dehumanize others like this, especially as the evil dehumanizes the perpetrators.

The Pocket Dictionary of Ethics puts it like this:

> Slavery is considered morally repugnant because it reduces a human person to the status of property thereby violating the slave's human rights and dehumanizing both master and slave.[27]

At one time in history, there were those who have attempted to use the Scriptures to justify the slave trade. John Henry Hopkins (1864) is reported to have penned the following words:

> The Bible's defense of slavery is very plain. St. Paul was inspired and knew the will of the Lord Jesus Christ and was only intent on obeying it. And who are we, that in our modern wisdom presume to set aside the word of God and invent for ourselves a higher law: than those holy Scriptures which are given to us as a light to our feet and a lamp to our paths in the darkness of a sinful and a polluted world?[28]

Swartley quotes Dwight Weld, who speaks on behalf of the slaves who struggle to find a voice for themselves.

> Slavery seeks refuge in the Bible only in its last extremity. Goaded to frenzy in its conflicts with conscience and common sense, it courses up and down the Bible, seeking rest and find none. The law of love, glowing on every page, flashes through its anguish and despair.

---

27. *Pocket Dictionary of Ethics*, 109.
28. Swartley, *Slavery, Sabbath, War and Women*, 31.

Here the golden rule is described as the Law of Love. Paul re-echoes the same message when he states, "Love does no harm to a neighbor. Therefore, love is the fulfillment of the law" (Rom 13:10). When we read these injunctions we recognize that today there are also other ways in which people sometimes seek to enslave people – through drug abuse, prostitution and even something seemingly as innocent as online gaming.

Woolman is reported to have uttered a prayer that resonates well with us:

> I have seen in the light of the Lord that the day is approaching when the man that is most wise in human policy shall be the greatest fool; and the arm that is mighty to support injustice shall be broken in pieces.[29]

---

29. John Woolman, "The Journal of John Woolman" in *The Inward Pilgrimage* (ed) Bernard Christensen (Minneapolis: Augsburg Publishing House, 1996), 91.

Conclusion

The loss of love, truth, justice and unity has created room for corruption and other forms of moral decadence. Greed and obsession with material wealth and political power have imprisoned Nigerians and their leaders in a sea of corruption. As a result, today Nigeria is part of a world that has essentially lost these moral and ethical ingredients that keep life together. Human dignity has been replaced by monetary value.

As the most populous black nation on the continent, Nigeria feels that God has given it the power and authority to be "the big brother" of Africa. However, we have to acknowledge with embarrassment that Nigeria has failed in its duty because of the massive corruption among its elite groups—the military, the politicians and the public servants. Love, truth, justice and unity have been forgotten in the rush to success.

Clearly Nigerian corruption is a systemic problem – an embedded corporate culture of making a profit without any regard for the impact on one's compatriots. This corporate culture is driven by fear, self-interest, greed, an obsession with socio-political and socio-economic power and a belief that material wealth is all that matters.

I therefore call on the religious communities in Nigeria to examine their faith, their ethics and their morality. To do so, the church will need to reflect deeply and to confess openly. Moreover, I believe that the Nigerian church must take the lead in inter-religious dialogue, in a Christ-like spirit of love, truth, justice and unity so that the impact of our call echoes across the land.

And finally, a prayer for our country:

O Lord, as our moral feet here in Nigeria are slipping away from what you desire, from love, truth, justice and unity, hear our cry. We long for the restoration of love, truth, justice and unity so that our country can be united as one people, whether we come from the north or south, from the west or east or from the central provinces. Come, O Lord and change our hearts.

Bibliography

Accra Charter of Religious Freedom and Citizenship." *International Bulletin of Missionary Research 35/4*, (2011). https://religiousfreedom.yale.edu/sites/default/files/files/Accra%20Charter%20and%20Introduction.pdf

Achebe, Chinua. *An Image of Africa and the Trouble with Nigeria*. London: Penguin Group, 1983.

Adaku, Nwauzor. "Changing Values in Contemporary Nigeria" in *Educational Research International* Vol. 3 (1) February 2014.

Adedigba, Timothy Adewole & Wahab, Elizabeth Ikeola. "Degenerated Moral Values in Nigeria: Challenges of Social Studies Education." *Nigerian Journal of Social Studies*, Vol. 8/1 (April, 2015): 37–49.

Agang, Sunday Bobai. *The Impact of Ethnic, Political, and Religious Violence on Northern Nigeria, and a Theological Reflection on Its Healing*. Carlisle, Cumbria: Langham Monographs, 2011.

Agang, Sunday Bobai, Pillay Pregala, Jones, Chris. eds. *A Multi-Dimensional Perspective on Corruption in Africa: Wealth, Power, Religion and Democracy*. Cambridge: Cambridge Scholars Publishing, 2019.

Agbese, Dan. *Nigeria Their Nigeria*. Ikeja, Lagos: Newswatch Books Ltd, 2008.

Allison, Gwendoline. "Respect in the Workplace", http://www.lgma.ca/assets/Chapter~Information/North~Central/Valkyrie~Attachments~Sept~2012~Conf/Respect-in-the-Workplace.pdf

Amponsah, Kwabena. *Topics on West African Traditional Religion*. Legon, Accra: Adwinsa Ghana Ltd., 1977.

Amujuri, B.A., Agu, S.U. & Onodugo, Ifeanyi Chris, "Is Nigeria's Claim of Leadership Role in Africa a myth or Reality"? International Journal of Multidisciplinary Research and Development, 2/7 (2015): 343–353. http://www.allsubjectjournal.com/download/1043/2-6-33.pdf

Appiah, Kwame Anthony. "Mistaken Identities: Creed, Country, Color, Culture." BBC Reith Lectures 2016. http://www.bbc.co.uk/programmes/b080t63w

Awolowo, Obafemi. *Voice of Courage*, Vol.1. Lagos, Nigeria: Fagbamigbe Publishers, 1981.

Baranzke, H. "The Sanctity of Human Life" https://link.springer.com/article/10.1007/s10677-012-9369-0.

Bellah, Robert M., Madsen, Richard, Sullivan, William M., Swidler, Ann and Tripton, Steven M. *Habit of the Heart: Individualism and Commitment in American Life*. Berkeley, Los Angeles: University of California Press, 1996.

Birnbacher, Dieter. "Moral and Other Values" in *Kultura Wartosci* No. 4(8) July 2013. www.philosophica.ugent.be/fulltexts/39-6.pdf.

Bishop, Craig and Bishop, Matthew T. *Faithspace in the Workplace*. Harleysville, PA: BranchCreek Community Church, 2005.

Blake, M. "Voices of a Nation: Recent Recordings from South Africa." *South African Music Studies*, 26–27/1 (2006): 145–159.

Boer, Jan H. *Christianity and Islam under Colonialism in Nigeria*. Jos: ICS, 1988.

———. *Nigeria's Decades of Blood: 1980–2002*: Studies in Christian-Muslim Relations. Vol. 2. Jos: Stream Christian Publishers, 2004a.

———. *Why This Muslim Violence*: Studies in Christian-Muslim Relations. Vol. 3. Jos, Nigeria: MoreBooks, 2004b.

Çancı, Haldun and Odukoya, Opeyemi Adedoyin. "Ethnic and Religious Crises in Nigeria: A specific analysis upon identities (1999–2013)." *African Journal on Conflict Resolution* 16/1 (2016): https://www.accord.org.za/ajcr-issues/ethnic-religious-crises-nigeria/.

Chukwu, K. U., Chukwu, E.A. and C. Chinedu-Oko. "Dialectics of Contradiction in Mother Earth and Fatherland: An Eco- Linguistic Examination of the Nigerian National Anthems," *FUTO Journal Series* 3/2 (2017): 225–234.

Cunliffe-Jones, Peter. *My Nigeria: Five Decades of Independence*. New York, NY: Palgrave Macmillan Publishers, 2010.

Dogo, Sefinatu Aliyu. "The Nigerian Patriarchy: When and How," *Cultural and Religious Studies* 2/5 (2014): 263–264.

Dow E., Philip. *Virtuous Minds: Intellectual Character Development*. Downers Grove, Illinois: IVP Academic, 2013.

Edwards, Joel. *An Agenda for Change: A Global Call For Spiritual and Social Transformation*. Grand Rapids, Michigan: Zondervan, 2008.

El-Rufai, Nasir Ahmad. *The Accidental Public Servant*. Ibadan: Safari Books Ltd, 2013.

Ezenweke, Elizabeth Onyedinma, and Nwadialor, Loius Kanayo. "Understanding Human Relations in African Traditional Religious Context in the Face of Globalization: Nigerian Perspectives", *American International Journal of Contemporary Research, Vol. 3 No. 2*, (February 2013): 61–70.

Faniyan, Gabriel. "A Stylistic Analysis of the Nigerian National Anthem and Pledge." https://gabrielfaniyan.wordpress.com/2012/08/07/a-stylistic-analysis-of-the-nigerian-national-anthem-and-pledge/.

Fergusson, Everett. *Backgrounds of Early Christianity*. 2nd ed., Grand Rapids: Wm B. Eerdmans Publishing Company, 1993.

Glass, Zipporah G. "Land, Slave Labor and Law: Engaging Ancient Israel's Economy" Journal for the Study of the Old Testament, JSOT 91 (2000).

Gooding, David W. and John Lennox. *The Bible and Ethics*. Myrtlefield Trust, 2015

Heidelberg Catechism, crcna.org/sites/default/files/HeidelbergCatechism.pdf

Holmes, Arthur F. *Ethics: Approaching Moral Decisions*. Leicester: Intervarsity Press, 1984.

Ibrahim, J. and Kazah-Toure, T. *Ethno-Religious Identities in Northern Nigeria*. Uppsala: Nordic Africa Institute, 2003.

Ijatuyi-Morphé, Randee. *Africa's Social and Religious Quest: A Comprehensive Survey and Analysis of the African Situation.* Jos: Logos-Quest Publishing, 2011.

Joshua, Segun, Ronald E. Loromeke and Ilemobola P. Olanrewaju, "Quota System, Federal Character Principle and Admission to Federal Unity Schools: Barriers to Learning in Nigeria," *International Journal of Interdisciplinary and Multidisciplinary Studies* (IJIMS) 2/2 (2014): 1–10.

Kalu, Viktor Eke. *The Nigerian Condition: Arthur Nwankwo's Viewpoints and Blueprints.* Enugu: Fourth Dimension Publishers, 1986.

Kreeft, Peter. *Back to Virtue: Traditional Moral Wisdom for Modern Moral Confusion.* San Francisco, CA: Ignatius Press, 1997.

Krznaric, Roman. *How Should We Live?: Great Ideas from the Past for Everyday Life.* Katonah, New York: BlueBridge, 2013.

Kukah, Matthew Hassan. *The Church and the Politics of Social Responsibility.* Ikate-Surulere, Lagos: Sovereign Prints Nig Ltd, 2007.

Kunhiyop, Samuel Waje. *African Christian Ethics.* Bukuru: Africa Christian Textbooks, 2008.

Lee, Kuan Yew, *From Third World to First.* New York: HarperCollins, 2000.

Maier, Karl. *This House Has Fallen: Nigeria in Crisis.* Colorado: Westview Publishers, 2000.

Magagula, C.M. "Conflict Resolution and Management: The Role of African Higher Education Institutions." 2008: http://www2.ncsu.edu/ncsu/aern/confma.html.

Mangalwadi, Vishal. *Truth and Transformation: A Manifesto for Ailing Nations.* Seattle, W.A: YWAM Publishing, 2009.

Marshall, Monty G. *Conflict Trends in Africa, 1946–2004: A Macro-Comparative Perspective.* Arlington: Center for Global Policy, 2005.

Mbah, Mazi C.C. *Government & Politics in Modern Nigeria: The Search for An Orderly Society.* Onitsha, Nigeria: Joanee Educational Publishers Ltd, 2001.

Michael, Matthew. "Liberation in Exodus and Quest for Peace in Africa: Beyond the Rhetoric of Liberation and the Mapping of Peace in Exodus." In *Sapientia Logos: A Journal of Biblical Research & Interpretation in Africa* 7/1 & 2 (2015):

Mohammed, Iliyasu Biu and Evans, Oluwagbamila Ayeni. "Political Leadership in Nigeria: Our National Anthem and National Pledge." *Africology: The Journal of Pan African Studies* 12/1 September (2018):

Moltmann, Jurgen. *God for a Secular Society: The Public Relevance of Theology,* Minneapolis: Fortress Press, 1999.

Moyser, George. *Politics and Religion in the Modern World.* ed. London: Routledge, 1991.

Munther, Isaac. *From Land to Lands, From Eden to the Renewed Earth.* Carlisle: Langham Monograph, 2015.

Njoku, Donatus I. "Re-Orientation of Value System in Nigeria: A Critic." *Global Journal of Arts, Humanities and Social Sciences,* Vol.3, No. 11, (November, 2015): 25–32.

Nnoli, Okwudiba. *Ethnic Politics in Nigeria.* Enugu: Fourth Dimension, 1976.

Noyoo, N. "Ethnicity and Development in Sub-Saharan Africa." *Journal of Social Development in Africa,* 15/2 (2000):

Nwaomah, S.M. "Religious Crises in Nigeria: Manifestation, Effect and the Way Forward." *Journal of Sociology, Psychology and Anthropology in Practice* 3/2, (2011):

Nwaubani, O. O. "Values Clarification Strategies and Students' Performance in Some Values Concepts in Social Studies." PhD diss., University of Ibadan, 1996.

Obasanjo, Olusegun. *This Animal Called Man.* Ogun, Nigeria: ALF Publication), n.d

Ogbeidi, M.M. "Political Leadership and Corruption in Nigeria Since 1960: A Socio-Economic Analysis." *Journal of Nigeria Studies* 1, (2012):

Ogunsanwo, Olufemi. *General Yakubu Gowon: The Supreme Commander.* Oxford: African Books Collective Ltd., 2009.

Okobia, Faith Nkem, Okafor, Mary I & Osajie, Justina M, "Reactivating Nigerian Norms and Values through Religious Studies for National Transformation." Vol 12 (2016). *African Journals Online* (AJOL) http://dx.doi.org/10.4314/og.v12i s1.10.

Oji, Mazi Kanu. *The Nigerian Ethical Revolution 1981–2000 AD.* Lagos: Federal Secret Printers, 1982.

———. *The Action Phase of the Nigerian Ethical Revolution 1981–2000 AD.* Lagos: Mazi Kanu Oji Publishers, 1985.

Okai, M. O. "The Role of the Christian Church in Conflict Management in the Niger Delta Region of Nigeria." PhD diss. Graduate School, University of Calabar, Calabar, 2007.

Okonjo-Iweala, Ngozi. *Reforming the Unreformable: Lessons From Nigeria.* Cambridge and London: The MIT Press, 2012.

———. *Fighting Corruption is Dangerous: The Story Behind the Headlines.* Cambridge: The MIT Press, 2018.

Olaniyi, Kaseem. "Politeness Principle and Ilorin Greetings in Nigeria: A Sociolinguistic Study" in *International Journal of Society, Culture & Language,* 5(1), (2017). http://ijscl.net/article_24931_3dbd4a7da53b6a9e00d0870afa3bb8e9.pdf.

Olawoyin, Oladeinde. "Perception of Corruption Worsens in Nigeria: Transparency International Report" *Premium Times* February 22, 2018, *https://www.premiumtimesng.com.*

Olowolaju, P. S. "The Work Ethic of Nigerian Workers and Its Effects on Productivity." globalacademicgroup.com/journals/the%20nigerian%20academic%20forum/Olowolaju22.pdf.

Onditi, Francis. "African National Anthems: Their Value System and Normative 'Potential,'" African Study Monographs, Suppl. 56, March (2018).

Ortner, Sherry. "Is Female to Male as Nature is to Culture?" Feminist Studies 1 (1972): 5–31.

———. *Making Gender: The Politics and Erotics of Culture.* Boston: Beacon Press, 1996

Osaghae, Eghosa E. and Suberu, Rotimi T. "A History of Identities, Violence, and Stability in Nigeria." CRISE Working Paper No. 6. Oxford: Centre for Research on Inequality, Human Security and Ethnicity. https://assets.publishing.service. gov.uk/media/57a08c9840f0b652dd00141e/wp6.pdf

Osunwokeh, Clement I. "Human Dignity Stance of Umunna Solidarity in Igbo Traditional Society: A Challenge to African Christianity," *Journal of Scientific Research & Reports Vol. 8 No. 2*, (2015): 1–11.

Otite, Onigu and Isaac, Albert O. *Community Conflicts in Nigeria: Management, Resolution and Transformation*. Ibadan: Spectrum, 1999.

Oyugi, W.O. "Ethnicity in the Electoral Processes: The 1992 General Election in Kenya." African Association of Political Science 2/1 (1997).

Palmer-Jones, Nancy and Pat Hoertdoerfer. "Let's Talk About Respect". https://www. uua.org/files/documents/hoertdoerferpat/respect.pdf.

Pierri, Zacharias and Barkindo, Atta. "Muslims in Northern Nigeria: Between Challenge and Opportunity." https://www.researchgate.net/publication/310596098

Rae, Scott B. *Moral Choices: An Introduction to Ethics*. Grand Rapids, Michigan: Zondervan Publishing House, 1995.

Rosaldo, Michele and Louise Lamphere, eds., *Women, Culture and Society*. Stanford: Stanford University Press, 1974.

Rutland, Mark. *Character Matters: Nine Essentials Traits You Need to Succeed*. Florida: Charisma House, 2003.

Saha, S.C. "Ethnicity as a Resilient Paradigm: Socio-Political Transition and Ethnic Conflict in Africa." *Social Evolution and History* 9/1 (2000):

Sider, Ronald J. *The Scandal of Evangelical Politics*. Grand Rapids, Michigan: Baker Books, 2008.

Siollun, Max. *Oil, Politics and Violence: Nigeria's Military Coup Culture (1966–1976)*. New York: Algora Publishing, 2009.

Sparks, Kenton L. "The Egalitarian Spirit in Biblical Law" in *Sapientia Logos*: A Journal of Biblical Research and Interpretation in Africa 1/1 (2008):

Stonawski, Marcin, Potančoková, Michaela, Cantele, Matthew and Skirbekk, Vegard "The changing religious composition of Nigeria: Causes and Implications of Demographic Divergence." *Journal of Modern African Studies* 54/3, 2016:

Swartley, Willard M. *Slavery. Sabbath, War and Women: Case Issues in Biblical Interpretation*. Ontario: Herald Press, 1983.

Turaki, Yusufu. *The British Colonial Legacy in Northern Nigeria: A Social Ethical Analysis of the Colonial and Post-Colonial Society and Politics in Nigeria*. Jos: Yusufu Turaki Foundation, 1993.

———. *Tainted Legacy: Islam, Colonialism and Slavery in Northern Nigeria*. McLean VA: Isaac Publishing, 2010.

Tushima, Cephas T. A. *The Fate of Saul's Progeny in the Reign of David*. Eugene, OR: Pickwick Publications, 2011.

Unongo, Paul Iyorpuu. *Say It Loud: We're Black and Strong*. Shomolu, Lagos: Micho Commercial Printers, 1970.

Usuanlele, Uyilawa & Ibhawoh, Bonny eds. *Minority Rights and the National Question in Nigeria* Palgrave: Macmillan, 2017.

Ushe, M. U. "Role of Traditional African Moral Values in the Development of Nigeria" in *Journal of Sociology, Psychology and Anthropology in Practice*, Vol. 3. No. 2 (2011): 1–13.

Vaughan, Olufemi. *Religion and the Making of Nigeria*. Durham: Duke University Press, 2016.

Wa Kuhenga, Makwaia. "Africa: Slave Trade in Africa in the 21st Century?" *Tanzania Daily News,* December 2017. http://allafrica.com/stories/201712150738.html.

Warner, Zach. "The Sad Rise of Boko Haram." *New African* 01 April 2012.

Wright, Christopher J.H. *Old Testament Ethics for the People of God*. Nottingham: InterVarsity Press, 2004.

Yakubu, Alhaji M., Adegboye, R.T., C.N. Ubah, C.N. & Dogo, B. eds. *Crisis and conflict management in Nigeria since 1980*. Vol II. Kaduna: Nigerian Defence Academy, 2005.

Zecha, Gerhard. "The Golden Rule in Applied Ethics: How to Make Right Decisions in Theory and Practice." www.humanistica.roanuare/2011/Continut/Art%2006.pdf.

Zeleza, Paul T & Nhema, A (eds.) *The Roots of African Conflicts: The Causes and Costs*. Oxford: James Currey, 2008.

Langham
PARTNERSHIP

Langham Literature and its imprints are a ministry of Langham Partnership.

Langham Partnership is a global fellowship working in pursuit of the vision God entrusted to its founder John Stott –

to facilitate the growth of the church in maturity and Christ-likeness through raising the standards of biblical preaching and teaching.

Our vision is to see churches in the Majority World equipped for mission and growing to maturity in Christ through the ministry of pastors and leaders who believe, teach and live by the word of God.

Our mission is to strengthen the ministry of the word of God through:
* nurturing national movements for biblical preaching
* fostering the creation and distribution of evangelical literature
* enhancing evangelical theological education

especially in countries where churches are under-resourced.

Our ministry

Langham Preaching partners with national leaders to nurture indigenous biblical preaching movements for pastors and lay preachers all around the world. With the support of a team of trainers from many countries, a multi-level programme of seminars provides practical training, and is followed by a programme for training local facilitators. Local preachers' groups and national and regional networks ensure continuity and ongoing development, seeking to build vigorous movements committed to Bible exposition.

Langham Literature provides Majority World preachers, scholars and seminary libraries with evangelical books and electronic resources through publishing and distribution, grants and discounts. The programme also fosters the creation of indigenous evangelical books in many languages, through writer's grants, strengthening local evangelical publishing houses, and investment in major regional literature projects, such as one volume Bible commentaries like *The Africa Bible Commentary* and *The South Asia Bible Commentary*.

Langham Scholars provides financial support for evangelical doctoral students from the Majority World so that, when they return home, they may train pastors and other Christian leaders with sound, biblical and theological teaching. This programme equips those who equip others. Langham Scholars also works in partnership with Majority World seminaries in strengthening evangelical theological education. A growing number of Langham Scholars study in high quality doctoral programmes in the Majority World itself. As well as teaching the next generation of pastors, graduated Langham Scholars exercise significant influence through their writing and leadership.

To learn more about Langham Partnership and the work we do visit **langham.org**

www.ingramcontent.com/pod-product-compliance
Lightning Source LLC
Chambersburg PA
CBHW062113080426
42734CB00012B/2843